Lon

Pub Guide

CAMRA
BOOKS

CAMRA's London Pub Guide

Edited by Lynne Pearce

Cover design by McKie Associates
Cover photography by Keith Mayhew
Illustrations by Everet McKie

Maps by Perrot Cartographics
London maps taken from Collins Greater London Street Atlas, with the kind permission of HarperCollinsPublishers.
Base maps © Bartholomew Limited 2001

Printed by Albert Gait Limited, Grimsby

Published by CAMRA, The Campaign for Real Ale, 230 Hatfield Road, St. Albans, Herts AL1 4LW

Managing Editor: Mark Webb, mark-webb@msn.com

© CAMRA Ltd 2001

ISBN 1-85249-164-7

CONTENTS

3

INTRODUCTION

by Lynne Pearce

When I was first asked to write CAMRA's new guide to the capital's pubs, the request coincided with doing up my London flat, with the aim of making a fast buck and getting out while the going was good, to the Home Counties. How could I do a pub guide to a city I had grown tired of living in?

I'd lived in my bit of London since I'd been a student, moving to the capital from the Midlands in 1983 and, like so many of my contemporaries, never quite managing to find my way home again. As everyone will always tell you, almost I think to try to make you feel better about landing in your very small space in the great metropolis, London is a collection of "villages". Mine, where I'd lived for 17 years, at too many addresses to remember, was the rough side of one of London's poorest boroughs, Haringey. Here the more likely scenario is seeing refugees struggling to make ends meet on their food stamps, rather than tourists with their wads of cash to spend on tacky souvenirs. Not quite the stuff of dreams but it was bright lights, big city and the capital cast her spell upon me and persuaded me to stay.

Just like any other great capital city, London has the best and the worst of every-thing. From catwalk fashion to burgeoning crime statistics; dodgy street food to street credibility; a sense of history to the daily histrionics created by yet another transport cock-up – and, before we forget why we're here, the sustenance of life itself, beer and pubs a plenty.

When I embarked on this guide, my greatest worry was that I would be unable to find enough pubs worth reviewing. I'm delighted to say that my fears were unfounded. Of course there are too many ghastly theme bars, Oirish pubs and once lovely hostelries that have been allowed, through neglect or supposed progress, to fall into ruin – but the good news is that, in London at least, the great British pub is alive and well.

Whether the pubs included here have a history as long as your arm or are in the process of making their own reputation, my hope is that everyone who dips into this guide finds somewhere that entices them to step outside their front door and embark on an adventure. For who can predict whom you might meet, what you could see and the knowledge or fun you might find on the way?

As for me, in the process of compiling these suggestions, I discovered that I rather liked London after all. Her talent for change, and willingness to embrace new cultures and concepts, continually reinventing herself along the way, are but a handful of her enduring attractions. And what better place to consider what else she may offer than inside her many taverns? So what are you waiting for?

How to use this guide

I have a confession to make: I'm not the most ideal person to be asked to write a guide to London's finest hostelries, as possibly my least favourite way to experience pub culture is having a quick half in one pub whilst peering at the London A to Z, plotting the speediest way to get to the next. While I've had to do that, you, on the other hand, can do the opposite and my suggestion is that you savour the moment and take your time.

Pubs are arranged in their geographical areas, and grouped largely by their post-code rather than their proximity to each other. It's as well to bear in mind that whoever devised the London postcode system clearly had a good sense of humour, as the numbers bear little relation to logic. For example, you may think that SE6 would be more centrally located than SE16, but you'd be quite wrong, as the former borders Bromley in Kent, while you'll find the latter on the river. And unlike many other London pub guides, this one ventures into the outskirts of Greater London.

Many of the pubs I've included are the recommendations of CAMRA members, while others are more personal suggestions, based on my own experiences of living and working in the capital for almost two decades. The vast majority of entries include details like whether the pub is child-friendly, its accessibility for people with disabilities and how to get there by public transport. There's a guide to what the various symbols mean on page 9. And my advice is that if you're planning to visit a pub precisely because it offers a beer you've always wanted to try, it's child-friendly or you yearn for an English Sunday lunch or a Thai meal, it's worth ringing them beforehand to check that the status quo remains.

Before setting off, it's also a good idea to have a quick glance at a pub's opening hours, as although they can legally stay open all day and every day, many choose to close during weekday afternoons or may not open at all at the weekend. This is especially true of those pubs that are a bit off the beaten path or in specific areas, like the city of London, that in effect, shuts up shop from Friday evening through to Monday morning.

Inside these pages, you'll find pubs awash with history and others built in the last couple of decades; those with a no music policy and others that boast live bands every night of the week. Some major on a menu to rival the best of the city's restaurants, while in others you'll be lucky to be offered a choice of sandwiches at lunchtime. Probably the only thing these pubs share is that every one of them provides at least one real ale that's relatively well kept.

In short, my hope is that I've included as many different kinds and styles of pubs as there are potential pub-goers, giving everyone the chance to find something they like – and hopefully avoid what they don't. But there are two things to remember: the first is that one person's authentic, well-preserved pub may be another's flock-wallpapered, crime-against-taste nightmare. In other words, choice is always subjective.

And the second more important consideration is that, with the best will in the world, any guide can only ever be a snapshot in time. Things change and not always for the better. For instance, good publicans may be lured elsewhere, pub companies alter their real ale policies or the refurbishers move in and, as the Americans might say, "wreck the joint". In the few months it has taken me to compile this book, at least one pub I wished to include has closed down, while another is under threat of being turned into a pizza parlour. But you know precisely what you need to do to stop that happening again − visit the pub. Cheers.

KEY

✿ A garden or, where specified, other outdoor area for drinking – occasionally this will just be tables on the pavement.

♿ Disabled access to the premises.

🎠 A pub where the licensee will allow in children accompanied by a parent or other responsible adult. This symbol does not necessarily imply that the pub has a Children's Certificate; it may be a family room. Check with staff. See 'Children in Pubs'.

Ⓟ Parking available.

⊖ Nearest underground station. This will be just a few minutes walk unless otherwise stated in the text.

⇄ Near a railway station.

CAPITAL HISTORY

by Roger Protz

Think of London and several things spring to mind: history in abundance, a
mighty river, the Houses of Parliament, the dearly-departed Dome, seats of learn-
ing, financial institutions, black cabs and red buses. But London as a great brewing
centre? *Shurely shome mishtake,* as the capital's satirical magazine *Private Eye* is wont
to say.

Yet London does have a great brewing tradition. It was once, during the 18th and
early 19th centuries, the greatest brewing centre in the world. Porter and its
stronger brother stout were first brewed in London. They made fortunes for such
producers as Sam Whitbread, and transformed brewing from a cottage industry
into a large commercial one.

But today all the great names of London brewing – Charrington, Courage, Ind
Coope (just over the border in Essex), Truman, Watney and Whitbread – are long
gone. Of the giants, only Guinness remains at Park Royal, producing 'draught'
stout that is filtered, pasteurised and gaseous.

There is a welcome clutch of small breweries, several based in restaurants, but –
with the exception of the all-organic Pitfield and the Sweet William brew-pub –
they make mainly lager and filtered ales. The commercial brewing of real cask-
conditioned, copper-bottomed ale resides with the two family-owned companies
of Fuller's in Chiswick and Young's in Wandsworth. Splendid and honourable
though they are, Fuller's and Young's cannot quite turn London into a brewing
capital again.

London's brewing history

Breweries were not always so thin on the ground. In the 11th century, the
Domesday Book recorded that the monks of St Pauls' Cathedral brewed some
67,000 gallons of ale a year. When Henry VIII dissolved the monasteries, he
unwittingly encouraged the development of commercial brewing. Most tavern
owners brewed on the premises, but the demands from a growing population gave
rise to 'common brewers' who were not confined to ale houses. A Brewers'
Company was set up in 1437 to represent the interests of common brewers. The
company, with twenty-six members, was given a royal charter by Elizabeth I in
1560.

As commercial brewing developed, many plants were established on the banks of
the Thames. Brewers were not allowed access to the conduits that brought supplies of fresh drinking water to the capital. The Thames offered transport for
grain and hops as well as finished beer, while bore holes sunk alongside the river
tapped into supplies of pure water that were used as 'liquor' in the brewing
process. London's water, being relatively soft beneath clay soil, was ideally suited

to producing full-flavoured mild, porter and stout beers with the malty sweetness demanded by people engaged in heavy manual labour.

Porter transformed brewing in the early 18th century. It not only turned London into the undisputed capital of British brewing, but it also had a powerful impact on brewing processes throughout the world. Porter today is such a niche product confined mainly to small craft breweries in Britain and the United States that it is hard to grasp the sheer size of the London porter brewing market in the 18th and 19th centuries, with Barclay Perkins producing 270,000 barrels a year, Meux Reid 188,000, Truman Hanbury 150,000, and Whitbread 122,000.

At the turn of the 18th century, London drinkers favoured a beer known as three threads, a mix of brown, pale and 'stale' ales: stale was a beer matured in oak vats for a year or more that acquired a sour, lactic tang. Before the arrival of the beer engine that drew beer from cellar to bar, mixing three threads from different casks was a laborious business for tavern owners and their employees. A brewer in Shoreditch, Ralph Harwood of the Bell Brewhouse, brewed a beer in 1722 that reproduced the flavours of three threads but had the advantage of coming from just one cask. Harwood called his beer 'entire butt', but its popularity with London's street workers, in particular the vast army of porters who carried food from markets to shops and homes, soon gave it the nickname of 'porter'.

Brewing dynasties

Harwood's place in brewing history was assured, but he was soon eclipsed by such brewers as Sam Whitbread. Whitbread began his career as a brewer of pale and brown ales in a modest plant in Old Street in 1742. Within a few years he had moved to much larger premises in the Barbican and went over entirely (sic) to porter production. With London growing at a furious pace as land enclosures drove tens of thousands of dispossessed peasants into the city, the clamour for wholesome beer became insatiable. Sam Whitbread became the first member of the 'beerage', his portrait painted by Reynolds, a seat in parliament, and a large mansion in Hertfordshire.

Soon other brewing dynasties – Charrington, Barclay Perkins, Meux, and Truman – were vying for a slice of the porter market. They embraced all the new technologies of the Industrial Revolution, such as steam power, thermometers, hydrometers, iron mash tuns, enclosed coppers, and coke-fired rather than wood-fuelled kilns for malting, to produce porter in such vast amounts that ale-house brewers went into rapid decline.

It was the custom of the time to call the strongest beer in a brewery 'stout'. As a result, the most powerful porters were dubbed stout porters. Over time, these strong versions of porter became known simply as stout, especially when such Irish brewers as Guinness in Dublin, and Beamish & Crawford and the Murphy brothers in Cork developed their own versions of the style in a bid to stem the flood of London-brewed porter and stout into Ireland. Porter and stout production came to a virtual halt in Britain during World War One when the government banned the use of dark malts that required extra energy during the roasting process, energy that was needed by the munitions factories. But the style had already come under pressure early in the 19th century when pale ale burst on the brewing scene.

'India Ale', later known as India Pale Ale, was first brewed by Hodgson's Brewery at Bromley-by-Bow in East London. Using no coloured malts, Hodgson at the end of the 18th century fashioned a beer from pale malt with large amounts of hops that he exported to Bombay and Calcutta from the nearby East India Docks. The brewers in Burton-on-Trent, suffering from a collapse of their trade with the Baltic States as a result of the Napoleonic Wars, also began to brew pale ales, made possible by the invention of coke that enabled large amounts of cheap pale malt to be made. The Burton brewers found that the spring waters in the Trent Valley, rich in sulphates, were ideally suited to brewing pale beers with a natural sparkle, clarity in the glass and great hop character. Such brewers as Allsopp, Bass and Worthington quickly eclipsed Hodgson. Other London and Essex brewers, notably Charrington, Ind Coope (who eventually merged with Allsopp), Mann, Crossman & Paulin, and Truman established second breweries in Burton to take advantage of the waters. With the exception of Ind Coope, they did not enjoy great success in the Midlands and soon retreated back to London. When their scientists discovered how to 'Burtonise' London water by adding sulphates, they were able to brew pale ale without leaving home.

Twentieth century

By the second decade of the 20th century even mighty Whitbread had torn down its great porter vats and had gone over to mild and pale ale production. As the bigger brewers started to build large estates of 'tied pubs' – pubs directly owned by them – they moved away from vatted porters and IPAs to 'running beers' that cleared quickly in casks and gave them a faster return on sales. Cask-conditioned mild and bitter remained the dominant beer styles until the end of World War Two. The loss of many experienced London pub landlords during the war, either as a result of bombing during the Blitz or on military service, led to a drop in the quality of draught beer. Drinkers turned to bottle beer, a consumer move that encouraged the larger London brewers to switch from naturally-conditioned cask beers to 'keg beer' – filtered, pasteurised and heavily-carbonated beers, essentially bottled beers in bigger containers. The substantial investment in modern bottle and keg production lines turned the likes of Charrington, Watney and Whitbread in to 'super-regionals'. They had national aspirations, trunking their dead beers to all parts of the country.

In the 1960s, Bass expanded into a national giant, eventually swallowing Charrington. The large regionals either rushed to merge in order to compete with Bass, or became the drinks subsidiaries of global giants. Whitbread bought and closed down scores of smaller regionals, while Courage was taken over by Imperial Tobacco. And Watney, having bought Mann and Truman, joined forces with Grand Metropolitan.

The rush to go national robbed London of some of its most famous brewing names. Courage left London and has now merged with Scottish & Newcastle. Watney left brewing altogether in the 1990s and there were few mourners at the funeral. Whitbread turned its historic Barbican brewery into offices and a conference centre before selling its remaining breweries in 2000 to Interbrew of Belgium. In Romford, Ind Coope helped form Allied Breweries in the 1960s, which in the 1990s sold its breweries to Carlsberg – only Tetley in Leeds is left – and eventually its pubs to Bass and Punch Taverns. Ind Coope's massive mash tuns and coppers are now being used somewhere in the People's Republic of China but it's unlikely they are producing John Bull Bitter.

And so a great heritage was destroyed. Fortunately good beer survives in London, mainly courtesy of those doughty and determined brewers at Fuller's and Young's. Enjoy their fine beers, enjoy London's magnificent pubs, but spare a thought for what greater joys there could be if other brewers had put community before crude profit.

Roger Protz edits the CAMRA *Good Beer Guide* and is the chairman of the British Guild of Beer Writers. His book (with Clive La Pensée) on India Pale Ale traces in more detail the origins of the style in London (*Homebrew Classics: India Pale Ale*, CAMRA Books, £8.99).

HUNGRY CITIZENS

by Susan Nowak

Dining out in London used to be a joke, a subject of contempt to foreigners who would not mention our capital in the same breath as Paris, Rome or even New York. Not any more. London now has an international reputation for fine food and innovative, feisty chefs who grace our TV screens and have made eating the new sex.

But has food in London pubs progressed in the same way? Well, yes...and no.

Yes, London pubs now do food in a big way. And, yes, some of it is absolutely terrific. And some of it is absolutely dire.

True, we have emerged from the grim days of Scotch eggs, pickled onions and that strange era of chicken or scampi in a basket. But food in London's hostelries is still a lottery. I can take you to pubs in the fashionable heart of the city, next door to the culinary delights of Chinatown and the splendour of grand hotel restaurants, where they still serve factory produced chilli and lasagne.

London pubs also seem to be almost the last bastion of my pet hate, the hot food counter, where congealing trays of shepherd's pie or sausage 'n' mash stand exposed to cigarette smoke and flu germs...

This is also, of course, the place for pub owners to make money – hence the theme chains dishing up microwaved misery from identical menus that are more concept than substance.

Eating by era

In mediaeval London you could rely on a decent meal at an inn. Chaucer's pilgrims set out from a Southwark tavern where they enjoyed a hearty repast before their journey to Canterbury. And in 1669 diarist Sam Pepys was at the "Miter" inviting his friends to "a good chine of beefe ... with three barrels of oysters and three pullets".

Dickens' trenchermen tucked in to many superb pub meals though, significantly, not in London. In Victorian London, licensed premises became drinking dens – gin palaces where you went to get sozzled, not eat. So perhaps we have now come full circle – from boozer to gastropub! Around 12 years ago when I began editing CAMRA guide *Good Pub Food*, there was precious little of it in London. But one place stood out as a pioneer of real food and real ale – the White Horse at Parsons Green in Fulham. It was in my first guidebook under the redoubtable Sally Cruickshank and in every edition since, now under the management of her then co-conspirator Mark Dorber. Dedicated to an ever changing range of beers, and imaginative fresh food, this is a pub which not only creates an inspiring menu but Mr Dorber, a cellarman par excellence, enthusiastically promotes the relation-ship between beer and food.

From his kitchen emerge dishes such as vegetable tempura in beer batter, duck liver and pancetta salad with a Belgian beer dressing or poached peaches in raspberry beer. On his blackboard he chalks a list of his current beers with descriptions, suggesting which best accompany dishes on the menu.

So perhaps this is the right moment to mention publicans' seeming reluctance to give beer the place it deserves, on the dinner table as well as the bar. If restaurants are the right place to promote wine, then surely pubs are the place to promote our glorious beer styles?

It is a little surprising that pubs are so slow to cotton on, because we do now have award winning eating places in London which are not pubs but which are attracting diners in their droves to a beer and food culture. Belgo began it in Chalk Farm, followed by its huge underground eaterie in Covent Garden with nearly 200 Belgian beers and cuisine à la bière such as salmon in Hoegaarden or duck with blackcurrant beer.

Freedom Brewery now has brew restaurants in London where diners can see micro brew plants behind glass producing wheat beers, red beers, lagers, alongside modern British cuisine. There is two-storey Mash off Oxford Circus brewing a changing range of beers and serving superb food in a sophisticated restaurant. More recently The Porterhouse in Covent Garden opened, serving its own Dublin brewed porter and an oyster stout flavoured with real oysters, a beer used in its own pork and oyster stout sausages. Granted, these places may not be serving real ale as CAMRA defines it, but they are introducing freshly brewed beers with a distinctive flavour to a new audience and, more important, placing them in the food context. Surely London publicans could take a leaf from their book? After all, tourists who flock here to see our world famous London taverns and admire some of their stunning architecture, should surely be taught the pleasure of our beer styles in their rightful setting: the pub.

Ethnic and eccentric

The two main London brewers Young's and Fuller's do deserve credit for some capital pub food in the capital. Fuller's has achieved the remarkable feat in a teeming metropolis packed with every ethnic cuisine under the sun of opening successful Thai kitchens in some of its pubs.

These are not theme pubs serving centrally produced bland Thai dishes, but individual diners with real cooks, many of them Thai, producing freshly made, authentic food. And as we know, it goes best with beer and lager. Young's encourages a catholic range of dining styles in its pubs. In Bruton Place just off Berkeley Square, for instance, there is The Guinea – perhaps the place Dickens' trenchermen might feel most at home.

In a panelled dining room reminiscent of a gentlemen's club they serve traditional British cuisine, especially fine Aberdeen Angus beef, and in particular the UK's most "decorated" steak and kidney pie originated by landlord Carl Smith, winner of more national "kate and sidney" pie competitions than any other.

But a pub favouring sassy, modern cuisine is also Young's – the Chelsea Ram in Burnaby Street near Chelsea harbour where I have enjoyed treats such as crab risotto cakes and sausage patties with horseradish mash.

And with a style different again are the Gottos, running three Young's pubs in London, and supplying them with home – grown meat raised on their farm in Surrey – an impressive way of bringing country produce direct into the capital. To my mind, too few London pubs achieve the standard of cooking of their rural colleagues – even though they still have the great London markets on their doorsteps.

And, talking of markets, Smithfield can offer something restaurants cannot. Pubs around the great meat market not only dish up magnificent breakfasts down to the black pudding and devilled kidneys, but can serve ale as early as 7.30am, a concession originally for the market porters.

London also has two organic pubs, foodie sister pubs the Duke of Cambridge in St Peter's Street, Islington, and The Crown in Grove Road, Bow, obtaining fresh produce from small suppliers and serving such treats as roast pheasant with olive mash, pumpkin and roast pepper risotto, and baked smoked haddock with leek mash and cheese sauce. Alongside are organic beers including Pitfield's Eco Warrior and Black Eagle, and St Peter's Organic Ale.

I believe London pubs should be a showcase for the best in food and beer. It can be a simple ploughman's, a Japanese tempura or a clever chef's subtle creation; it matters not as long as the dish is freshly prepared from quality ingredients offering good value for money.

Pub food in the capital is indeed a broad church. That must be why some is so heavenly – and some sheer hell!

Susan Nowak is editor of CAMRA guide *Good Pub Food*, and CAMRA recipe book *Pub Superchefs*, and author of *The Beer Cook Book*.

REAL ALE

What is real ale?

Real ale is a definition accepted by the Concise Oxford Dictionary. It is also known as traditional draught beer or cask-conditioned beer. Real ale is brewed from malted barley, using pure water and hops, and fermented by top-fermenting yeast. At the end of fermentation the beer is allowed to condition for a few days and is then racked into casks, often with the addition of priming sugar and a handful of dry hops for aroma. The beer continues to 'work' or ferment in the cask while a clearing agent called finings drags the yeasty deposits to the floor of the cask. The beer is neither filtered nor pasteurised and must not be served by any method using applied gas pressure.

Real ale can be served straight from the cask and many country pubs still use this method, while some special winter brews in town pubs are often dispensed from a cask on the bar. But most real ale is drawn – hence the word 'draught' – by a suction pump from the pub cellar. The pump is operated either by a handpump, a tall lever on the bar, or by an electric pump. Electric pumps are rare in the south of England but are used widely in the Midlands and the North.

Real ale should be served at a temperature of 55-56 degrees F (12-13 degrees C). This is a cool temperature that brings out the best characteristics of a top-fermented beer. It is a higher temperature than those used for serving lager beers, but it is pure bunkum that real ale is 'warm'.

Cask breather

Some pubs in this guide have a note attached explaining that the landlord dispenses the beer using a cask breather. CAMRA is very keen for landlords to provide point of sale labelling so that customers are aware of the style of dispense available. This effects the presentation and taste of the beer.

A poor replacement for good cellar management., a cask breather is a device that allows the beer drawn from a cask to be replaced by CO_2 at atmospheric pressure. The cask breather is used to maintain the condition of beers that have to remain in cask for more than a few days. Also known as a demand valve or aspirating valve.

ACKNOWLEDGEMENTS

For mom, who always had faith in me, dad, who gave me something to strive towards and most of all, Mark.

No book is ever produced by one person. My list of thanks is almost endless but must include: Cress at CAMRA HQ for her patience, humour in the face of adversity and uncanny ability to predict what might be needed next; Roger for his unstinting support, friendship and sound advice; Michael and Shani for talking me down from the ceiling through various technical disasters, going beyond the call of duty and doing far more than friends ought to ensure it happened; Jessie for putting up with it all; Deborah for swapping her usual large Chardonnay for a small glass of cask conditioned without complaining, proving her wizardry with headings and margins and being my BF and soul mate; Mark Turner for giving me the benefit of his wisdom at a particularly timely moment and Mark Webb for remaining calm, professional and listening. Last, but far from least, is my husband Mark, the Greater Bellied One, for plotting my course literally and metaphorically, enduring everything that went wrong and enjoying everything that went right, and being my port in a storm – I know I couldn't have done it without you.

I also owe a huge debt of gratitude to all the CAMRA members who e-mailed me and put pen to paper to share their favourite pubs with a wider audience, particularly Geoff in CAMRA's South West London branch for his tireless efforts on the book's behalf. And finally cheers to the many mates who were kind enough to accompany me on my travels, especially Liz, Marie and Dory. Yes it's my round.

CENTRAL LONDON

EC1

The Artillery Arms

102 Bunhill Row

Open: Monday-Friday: 11-11; Saturday: 12-11; Sunday: 12-10.30
Food: Monday-Friday: 12-3
 ♿ ✿
☏ *020 7253 4683*
Old Street or Moorgate tube
Beers: *Fuller's ESB, London Pride, Chiswick Bitter plus seasonal Fuller's Ales including Jack Frost, Summer Ale, Honey Dew and Red Fox. Brews from other breweries include: Arkells, Smiles, Everards, Jennings and St Peter's. Bottle conditioned beers include Fuller's 1845.*

As JJ, the landlord of this Fuller's pub says of his regulars: "They're not serious drinkers, but a clientele serious about their drink" and with a choice of five well-kept real ales always on offer, they can indulge their passion to the full.

Named after the Honourable Artillery Company (HAC), whose headquarters are nearby, there's been an inn on this site since 1702 and the current building dates from 1860. With its island bar and Victorian fireplaces, the Artillery Arms is a classic English pub, where city gents can be found rubbing shoulders with local students or soldiers from Armoury House. There's also an upstairs function room, which boasts a magnificent marble mantelpiece, while the walls are adorned with a series of aquatints depicting the HAC's history.

The pub is opposite the historic Bunhill Fields burial ground, the last resting place of such literary luminaries as Daniel Defoe, William Blake and John Bunyan and so near to the Barbican Centre that musicians from the orchestra might be found propping up the bar after a performance.

Food is traditionally English too and includes bangers and mash, a ploughman's and chicken, ham and leek pie. Vegetarians are catered for with pasta napolitana, veggie burgers and various sandwiches.

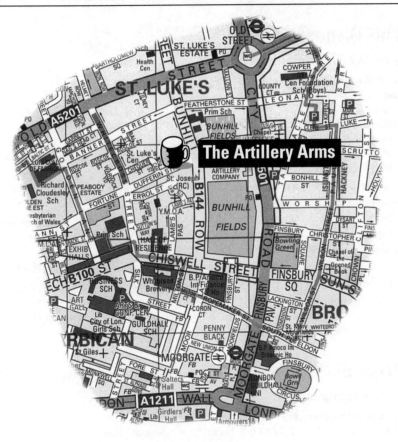

The Artillery Arms

The Bishops Finger

9-10 Westsmithfield

Open: Monday-Friday 11-11; closed Saturday and Sunday
Food: Monday-Friday 12-2.30 and 6-9
♿ ❧
✆ 020 7248 2341
Farringdon/Barbican/St Pauls tube; Bus 56
Beers: Shepherd Neame's Masterbrew, Spitfire, Bishop's Finger plus seasonal brews like Goldings, Late Red and Early Bird.

In addition to providing the range of Shep's ales, this small, two-storey Shepherd Neame pub has a justifiably good reputation for the originality of its food, worthy of being a previous star entry in CAMRA's *Good Pub Food* guide. As editor Susan Nowak writes: "A truly eclectic menu, offering the first home-made Japanese food and sushi I've had in a pub."

Choices might include yakisoba stir-fried vegetables with noodles and beer battered fresh haddock and fries, served with a pesto mayonnaise. Despite being next door to Smithfield's meat market, vegetarians get special treatment too, with homemade vegetarian ravioli and baked peppers filled with mushroom risotto amongst the suitable alternatives.

Britannia

94 Ironmonger Row

Open: Monday-Saturday: 11-11; Sunday: 12-10.30
Food: Monday-Friday: 12-3 and 6-9; Saturday: 6-9; Sunday: None
♿
✆ 020 7253 6441
Old Street tube
Beers: Boddingtons, Pedigree, Timothy Taylor's Landlord, Fuller's London Pride plus guest beers from Nethergate, Ridleys, O'Hanlons and others.

If you fancy a lively weekend, head for this pub on a Friday, Saturday or Sunday evening as it offers live music – or for those of a more cerebral nature, pit your wits at the pub quiz every Wednesday. During weekdays, the locals and tourists from the nearby hotel are more likely to be replaced with office workers.

A traditional English pub, set in the heart of London, there's a wide range of well-kept beers while food includes sirloin steak, roast chicken or lamb or, for non-meat eaters, vegetable lasagne.

Crown Tavern

43 Clerkenwell Green

Open: Monday-Friday: 11-11; Saturday: 12-11; Sunday: 12-5
Food: Monday-Friday: 12-3; Saturday: 12-4; Sunday: 12-5
& ❀ ➷ *at weekends*
Farringdon tube
☎ *020 7253 4973*
Beers: Tetley, Adnams, Fuller's London Pride, Bass plus guest beers from Brakspear, Greene King and Young's.

This traditional Victorian pub boasts a wealth of history in its well-maintained walls. Apparently built on the site of a medieval tavern that stood next to the London house of Oliver Cromwell, Lenin is said to have adjourned here for a quick snifter or two after a hard day studying the plight of the working classes at the nearby Marx Library. Others maintain that the pub is sited on the grounds of a nunnery. Certainly tunnels still run underneath that used to connect the Courthouse to the House of Detention.

All this historical speculation makes for thirsty work, so it's good to see that the Crown Tavern offers a wide range of cask conditioned beers, including a changing list of guest brews. Food includes hot sandwiches – like honey chicken – traditional pies, nachos, broccoli and potato bake and tortelloni Florentine.

A good venue when the heat is on, as customers can spill out on to the traffic free square at the front of the pub and make the most of the rare English sunshine.

Jerusalem Tavern

55 Britton Street, Clerkenwell

Open: Monday-Friday 11-11, closed Saturday and Sunday
Food: Monday-Friday 12-2.30
♿

☎ *01986 782322*

Farringdon tube; Liverpool Street mainline
Beers: this pub only stocks beers from St Peter's Brewery in Suffolk. At least six of the following are available on draft at any one time, with the remainder always available by the bottle: Wheat Beer, Best Bitter, Organic Ale, Golden Ale, Elderberry Beer, Old Style Porter, Honey Porter, Lemon and Ginger, Spiced Ale, Suffolk Gold, Summer Ale, Winter Ale, Organic Best, Strong Ale, Cream Stout, Grapefruit Beer.

For those of us who feel that a pub is more than just a place to while away a few hours, the Jerusalem Tavern could be considered a little slice of heaven. We pitched up to this tiny unprepossessing back street pub for a pint or two of St Peter's brewery beers on a cold, miserable December evening and were greeted with a warm welcome from helpful bar staff, smiling customers and even a real fire to melt the cockles of our hearts.

Once an 18th century coffee house, the pub retains all the cosy ambience you'd hope to find, helped along by candles dotted around on the half-a-dozen or so tables, distempered walls, tiles to covet and a bowed glass shop front dating from 1810. Crucially, there are no beeping games machines or piped muzak to spoil the illusion that you've stepped back to a slower paced time – and judging by the gentle buzz of conversation, permeated by the odd guffaw, clearly it's working.

Near to local landmark St John's Gate in Clerkenwell, part of the priory of St John, the Jerusalem Tavern is the only London-based, brewery owned outlet for the Suffolk brewers, St Peter's. I sampled the Wheat Beer while my better half chose the Organic Beer. Both were interesting and complex ales, beautifully kept. If you get the bug for this brewery's unusual beers, the pub can sell you a case of three each of four specially selected brews, all in their distinctively elegant green flasks.

Food is fairly basic but good quality and with a modern twist. Regular options include a locally made sausage selection, served in a crusty roll, sausage and mash with onion gravy or a ham, mushroom and cream cheese sandwich. For vegetarians, there is a brie and apple sandwich, served on walnut and raisin bread or an egg and cress sandwich served on olive bread.

My verdict: well worth a pilgrimage.

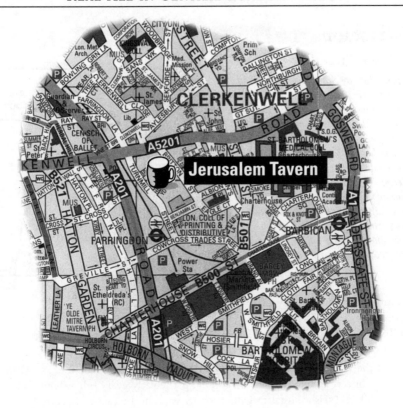

Jerusalem Tavern

O'Hanlons

8 Tysoe Street

Open: *Monday-Saturday: 11-11,*
Sunday: 12-10.30
Food: *Monday-Saturday: 12-2.30*
and 6-9.30, Sunday: 12-3
 ♿ ⛌
✆ *020 7278 7630*
Farringdon tube; Bus 38
Beers: *O'Hanlons Red Ale,*
Number One, Myrika, Harvey's
Best Bitter, Fuller's London Pride
plus seasonal beers from
Ecceshall, Crouch Vale,
Ringwood, Thwaites, York
Brewery.

So close to Sadler's Wells
Theatre that a particularly
sprightly ballet dancer could
probably leap from the stage and land pirouetting at the bar, O'Hanlons is that
rarest of London pubs – a proper Irish one.

Forget the Finnegan's faked Oirish theme bars, this one's as authentic as a Christy
Moore concert and almost as entertaining, particularly every other Thursday
when folk and Irish musicians gather for a session in the two-roomed pub.
Indeed, if you're a wizard with a tin whistle or you don't want to hang up your
harp, nip along as all are welcome to join in.

Décor is simple with scrubbed floorboards, wooden tables and benches, leaving
the eclectic clientele – who might include theatre-goers and workers from nearby
Amnesty International – to create the relaxed atmosphere that makes you want to
stay for just one more.

For devotees of the real stuff, the award-winning beers are a delight, lovingly created by John O'Hanlon at his Devon brewery, recently relocated from Vauxhall.
Food options include Ulster stew, Sunday roasts, salads and at least four veggie
dishes, including wild mushroom lasagne.

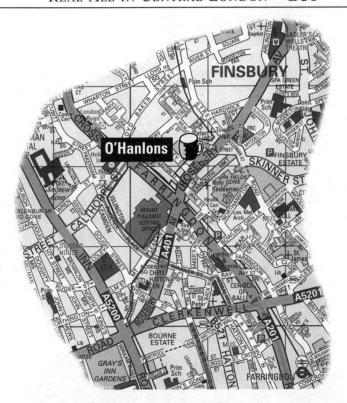

Old Red Lion

418 St John Street

Open: Monday-Friday: 11-11; Saturday: 12-3 and 7-11; Sunday: 12-3 and 7-10.30
Food: Monday-Friday: 12-3
♿ ❁ 🍼 *only before 7pm*
☏ *020 7837 7816*
Angel tube plus bus numbers 19, 30, 38, 43, 56, 73, 153, 214 and 341
Beers: Bass and Fuller's London Pride plus guest beers from Adnams, Young's, Greene King, Everards and Marston's.

Looking at the bumper to bumper traffic, jostling for space with the trendily clad citizens of this fashionable bit of London, it's hard to believe that Islington was once a country village – but that was the case in 1415, when the Old Red Lion was first built.

In the late Georgian era, the pub was described as a small brick house with three trees in its forecourt and, according to pub legend, it was in the shade of these trees that Thomas Paine, the radical political pamphleteer, wrote "The Rights of Man", a justification of the French Revolution. However, others argue that in fact he wrote his famous tract in the American colonies.

The present building dates back a mere 100 years to 1899. The pub has an usual layout, which has thankfully escaped "refurbishment", with a wood and engraved glass screen dividing the front area from the larger section. Built with two exits emerging on to different streets, the pub became known colloquially as the "In and Out" because cab passengers used to sometimes avoid paying their fare by entering the pub through one door and making a swift exit through the other.

Today, this is a thriving fringe theatre bar, hosting an innovative and diverse programme of plays, many of which premiere here. As a result it attracts more than its fair share of luvvies, including some famous faces who have made it into the big time and are here to show their support for those so far less fortunate.

After 22 years behind the bar, Tony and Pauline Sheriff-Geary retired last year but the pub is now in the capable hands of sister and brother team, Rebecca and Michael McCarthy, who are both CAMRA members. Already things are looking promising as they've introduced a guest beer and extended their licensing hours to include Sundays. Food includes staples like steak and ale pie, a curry, gammon, various sandwiches and salads and it's keenly priced, in contrast to many nearby Islington eateries.

Sekforde Arms

34 Sekforde Street

Open: Monday-Friday: 11-11; Saturday: 11-6; Sunday: 12-4
Food: Monday-Friday: 12-9.30; Saturday: 12-3.30; Sunday: 12-2.30
✿ ☞ restaurant only
☎ 020 7253 3251
Farringdon/Angel tube
Beers: Young's Bitter, Young's Special and Young's Triple A

This small street corner family local seems to make it into the pages of CAMRA's *Good Beer Guide* more often than not, so it must be doing something right. Bought by Young's brewery back in the 1980s, the name comes from Thomas Sekforde or Seckforde, a patron of Saxton the cartographer, a lawyer and Master of the Rolls, who retired to a house in the area.

Food is likely to include meat and vegetable lasagne, plaice, cod, scampi, gammon and rump steaks and, for the non-meat eaters, vegetable burgers and vegetarian sausages. And another plus – there's no jukebox.

The Viaduct Tavern

126 Newgate Street

Open: Monday-Saturday: 11-11;
closed on Sunday
Food: all day Monday to Saturday
St Pauls tube and all buses running
to and from Oxford Street
☎ 020 600 1863
Beers: Tetley, Fuller's London Pride,
Greene King IPA plus seasonals
and guests including Timothy
Taylor's Landlord, Hopback's
Summer Lightning and Waggle
Dance.

Sticking to the straight and narrow might be a good idea in the
Viaduct Tavern as the most
famous – or infamous, depending on which side you're on –
law court in the capital, the Old Bailey, is just over the road.

The pub is one of the few Victorian gin palaces still in its original form. Authentic features include a copper ceiling, three Victorian paintings depicting the statues from the Holborn Viaduct and gold and silver edged mirrors. The original ticket booth still remains intact behind the bar and there are moulds of faces, intended to represent the 16 hanging judges of the Old Bailey, adorning the stone reliefs. Another distinction is that it was the first public building in London to have an electric lighting system and there's also a debtors' prison, dating from 1775, in the cellars, so it's probably best to avoid asking for credit at the bar. Now owned by Nicholson's, food options include the ubiquitous bangers and mash, steak and ale pie and roast vegetable lasagne. Note that a cask breather is usually used on most real ales.

Ye Olde Mitre

1 Ely Court, Ely Place, Charterhouse

Open: Monday-Friday: 11-11; closed Saturday and Sunday
Food: Monday-Friday; 11-9.30
❦
Chancery Lane tube
☎ *020 7405 4751*
Beers: Friary Meux, Burton Ale and Tetley

Unfortunately the difficulties of finding this pub – tucked away down a narrow alleyway in a tiny courtyard between numbers eight and nine Hatton Garden, Ely Place – didn't deter the Christmas office party we stumbled over on our visit to this otherwise charming tavern.

The small historic pub, with its oak panelling and beams, is a careful 18th century replica of the original inn built in 1546 by Bishop Goodrich for the servants of his palace in Ely Place, used by the bishops of the cathedral of Ely in Cambridgeshire as their London base. The back room has another leading off it – where our Christmas revellers were to be found – and there's a smaller front bar. There are no gaming machines or music. Food is a variety of toasted sandwiches, all priced at £1.50.

EC2

Dirty Dicks

202 Bishopsgate

Open: Monday-Friday: 11-10.30; closed Sat; Sunday: 12-3
Food: Monday-Friday; 12-2.30
♿
Liverpool Street Station
☎ *020 7283 5888*
Beers: The Young's range including Special, Triple A and, from October to March, Winter Warmer. Bottle conditioned beer, Special London Ale, is also available.

Dirty Dicks has the dubious distinction of being the first London pub I ever visited, while on a sixth form trip from the Black Country to the great metropolis to find out if the streets really were paved with gold. Of course I discovered that the opposite was true, as my carefully saved pocket money disappeared in the blink of an eye, thanks to a quick stroll down nearby Petticoat Lane market.

Dating from 1870, the pub takes its name from Nathaniel Bentley, a City dandy who lived nearby in the late 18th and early 19th centuries. He was the unfortunate inspiration for the character of Miss Haversham in Charles Dickens' novel, "Great Expectations", as he was so stricken with grief when his fiancée died on the eve of their wedding that he shut the dining room, where their celebratory feast was to have been held, and left the contents to decay.

The poor tormented soul then allowed his appearance and everything around him to deteriorate, refusing to wash, change his clothes or clean his ironmonger's shop, eventually earning himself the nickname of Dirty Dick. When Bentley finally died in 1819, the landlord of the Old Port Wine Shop in Bishopsgate bought the shop, complete with grime and mummified cats, and moved them to his public house. Even when the pub was pulled down in 1870, the rotted memorabilia were kept for its replacement.

Thankfully for modern day customers and environmental health inspectors alike, today's pub is Dirty in name only. Owned by Young's brewery and serving the usual range of their beers, food includes pies, burgers and sausages. There's some imaginative options for vegetarians, for instance, fettucini with sun dried tomatoes and pesto and new potato, spinach and pine nut salad.

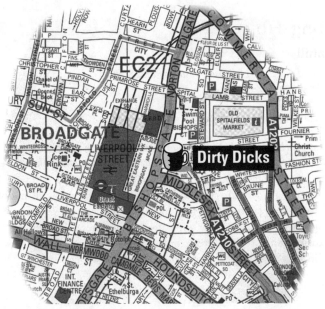

The Old Doctor Butler's Head

2 Masons Avenue, off Coleman Street

Open: Monday-Friday: 11-11; closed Saturday and Sunday
Food: Monday-Friday; 12-3
Bank tube
☎ *020 7606 3504*

Beers: Regulars include Boddingtons, Brakspear, Fuller's London Pride, Adnams, Wadworth's 6X and Flowers.

This is one of the oldest pubs in the city of London, dating back to 1616. Originally built by James 1's physician, Dr William Butler, at one time he was something of a one-man pub company, owning a dozen taverns in the capital. This is the last remaining pub of his mini empire.

With its low-beamed ceiling, wooden floor, oak panelling, mirrors and gas lighting, the pub is as traditional as you can get. There's a good range of beers regularly on offer, but the obliging publican will try to get anything that his customers request. Food veers towards the hearty and sustaining and includes steak and mushroom suet pudding, bangers and mash and roast of the day, which might be beef, turkey or pork. There also a vegetarian pie, lasagne and Stilton and mushroom bake.

EC3

Counting House

50 Cornhill

Open: Monday-Friday: 11-11; closed Saturday and Sunday
Food: Monday-Friday; 12-8
&

Bank, Liverpool Street, Fenchurch Street
☎ *020 7283 7123*

Beers: Regulars include Fuller's ESB, London Pride, Chiswick while seasonal and guest beers include Everard's Tiger and beers from Fuller's, Bateman and Adnams breweries.

The winner of an English Heritage Award in 1998, this grand pub with its large gallery overlooking a central island bar, used to be a bank. Now its marble walls and wood panelling play host to a thriving lunchtime crowd, who come to sample the range of Fuller's beers plus guests from other breweries, and the traditional menu, featuring fish and chips, steak and ale pie and various sandwiches. Nearby landmarks include the Bank of England and Mansion House.

Hoop and Grapes

47 Aldgate High Street

Open: Monday-Friday, closed Saturday and Sunday
Food: Monday-Friday 11-4
❀
Aldgate tube
☎ *020 7265 5171*

Beers: Regulars include Bass and Fuller's London Pride while the guest beer changes at least weekly and may be chosen from Adnams, Castle Eden, Badger or Timothy Taylor's Landlord.

For real ale fans this is an excellent venue as the pub offers up to 200 guest beers a year. Five minutes walk from Tower Bridge, reputedly it's the City's oldest pub, with foundations built in the 13th century and the present building dating from the late 1500s. Food is basic and includes burgers, bangers and pasta with some vegetarian alternatives.

The Hung, Drawn and Quartered

26-27 Great Tower Street

Open: Monday-Friday: 11-11; Saturday: 12-3.30; Sunday: 12-3, summer only
Food: Monday-Friday; 11-3.30; Saturday: 12-3; Sunday: 12-3, summer only
♿ ❀ ☒
Tower Hill tube; bus 15
☎ *020 7626 6123*

Beers: The Fuller's range including London Pride, ESB and Chiswick. Seasonal or guest beers might include Jack Frost, Honey Dew organic, Summer Ale and Red Fox.

A finalist in the Fuller's pub of the year contest in 1999, with a Cask Marque award and a Fuller's Master Cellarman rating, this is a pub that takes the quality of its beers very seriously indeed. The landlord's proud boast is that he sold almost 60,000 pints of real ale last year alone.

The pub is part of a Grade II listed building, which was originally the administration wing for Christ Church hospital. Catering for office workers and tourists, it's not hard to guess from the name that the pub is near to the Tower of London and Tower Bridge.

Food is freshly cooked and includes home made specials like ESB battered fish and chips and "a hangman's lunch" of mature cheddar or stilton, served with bloomer bread, salad and pickles. Vegetarian choices include farfalle with mixed peppers in an onion and leek sauce.

The Lamb Tavern

10-12 Leadenhall Market

Open: Monday-Friday: 11-9; closed Saturday and Sunday
Food: Monday-Friday
☙
Bank/Monument tube; buses 25, 47, 149, 35
☎ *020 7626 2454*
Beers: The Young's range including Special, Triple A and, from October to March, Winter Warmer.

During the 35 years the landlord, David Morris has been at the helm, his pub and the magnificent market have featured in several films starring such legendary actors as John Wayne, Robert Mitchum and, more recently, Russell Crowe, attracting showbiz and sports personalities to drop by for a quick pick-me-up. And if on your visit you don't manage to hunt down an autograph or two, at least there's the consolation of supping a well-kept pint of Young's beer before venturing off to peruse the wide range of foodstuffs available at the market's local delicatessens.

The Grade II listed Victorian tavern, close to the Tower of London and the Lloyds building, features masses of engraved glass and a tiled picture in the lobby of Sir Christopher Wren inspecting plans for the Monument, which marks the spot in Pudding Lane where the Great Fire of London broke out in 1666. There's a dive bar in the cellar, a mezzanine reached by a spiral staircase and a top floor bar – the first in London to become non-smoking – decorated with portraits of the directors of Young's brewery in Victorian Times.

The Lamb is also famous for its hot roast beef, available in French bread at lunchtimes, alongside pork or sausage. Vegetarians have a choice of salads.

EC4

The Old Bank of England

194 Fleet Street

Open: Monday-Friday: 11-11; closed Saturday and Sunday
Food: Monday-Friday: 12-8
Temple/Chancery Lane tube
☎ *020 7430 2255*
Beers: The Fuller's range, including London Pride, ESB and Chiswick, and Fuller's seasonal and guest beers, like Red Fox, Jack Frost, Summer Ale and Honey Dew.

Built in 1888 to house the Law Courts Branch of the Bank of England, the premises were sold in 1975 to a building society before Fuller's brewery took over the lease in 1994, undertaking a major refurbishment to restore the building to its former glory. Now there's an island bar, massive chandeliers dangle from the high ceilings and large windows enhance the grandeur, with the best views available from the mezzanine.

Food options include salmon and cod fishcakes, bangers and mash and rather daringly, given the grisly history of local pie-making, one made with steak and ale. The pub is near the site of Sweeney Todd's barber shop and it was in the tunnels and vaults below the present building that his victims were butchered before being cooked and sold in the pies of his mistress, Mrs Lovett, to unsuspecting customers. In the circumstances, you might want to plump for the vegetarian options of potato skins with mushrooms in garlic and cheese or the daily special.

The Old Bank of England

The Old Bell Tavern

95 Fleet Street

Open: *Monday-Friday: 11-11; Saturday: 12-6 and closed on Sunday*
Food: *Monday-Friday: 12-3*

❀ ☙

Blackfriars tube, City Thameslink and buses 4, 9, 11, 15, 26 and 74

☎ *020 7583 0216*

Beers: *Regular beers are Tetley, Bass, Brakspear and Timothy Taylor's Landlord and guests include Morland's Old Speckled Hen, Adnams Broadside and Young's Special.*

There's no piped music or a blaring jukebox to spoil the peace and tranquillity of this dimly lit, low-ceilinged pub that was built in 1670 for builders working on nearby St Bride's Church, badly damaged in the Great Fire of London and rebuilt by Sir Christopher Wren.

The 226 feet high elaborate spire of this church is said to be the inspiration for the traditional tiered English wedding cake. The church is also famous for its long association with the press and is known as the journalists' church. However, even in the days when Fleet Street was at the hub of the newspaper industry, I suspect that the majority of hacks were more likely to be found praising the secular delights of ale, than kneeling in the church pews.

Food at the Bell includes fish and chips, steak and ale pie and chicken and bacon ciabatta melt, while vegetarians might choose roast vegetable lasagne.

Ye Olde Cheshire Cheese

145 Fleet Street

Open: *Monday-Friday: 11.30-11; Saturday: 12-3 and 5.30 until 11; Sunday: 12-3*
Food: *Monday-Friday: 12-9.30; Saturday: 12-2.30; Sunday: lunch only*

☙

Blackfriars tube and buses 4, 11, 15, 23, 26 and 171.

☎ *020 7353 6170*

Beers: *Samuel Smith Old Brewery Bitter*

Amongst the most historic pubs in London, the Olde Cheshire Cheese is one of the capital's few remaining 17th century chophouses. The site formed part of the guesthouse of the 13th century Carmelite monastery and an inn has stood here since 1538. The present building was rebuilt after the Great Fire of London.

Here you can dine at the same oaken table reputedly used by Dr Johnson, Oliver Goldsmith and Charles Dickens, who mentions the inn in "A Tale of Two Cities". Other famous inhabitants have included Polly the parrot, who entertained visitors to the pub for 40 years. When she died, in 1926, the BBC broadcast the news and obituary notices appeared in more than 200 newspapers around the world.

Sadly much of the Cheese has suffered at the hands of the refurbishers, but the front room, complete with log fire, retains its olde-worlde charm. Food leans heavily towards the traditional with fish and chips, steak and kidney pudding and roast beef while vegetarians can enjoy nut wellington. Bear in mind that, although the pub serves real Sam Smith, the unconfirmed suspicion is that a cask breather is used.

Ye Olde Watling

29 Watling Street

Open: Monday-Friday: 11-11; closed Saturday and Sunday
Food: check times with licensee
🏵 🐎
Mansion House tube, Bow Lane Exit 4
☎ *020 7653 9971*
Beers: Regulars are Fuller's London Pride, Bass and Adnams Best Bitter while favourite seasonal and guests include Everard's Tiger and Harvey's beers.

Ye Olde Watling is next door to St Mary-le-Bow church, whose bells define whether or not you are a true London cockney, as legend has it that only those born within their sound can lay claim to the title. The pub was rebuilt in 1668 following the Great Fire of London, to offer hospitality to the workers rebuilding the damaged church.

Sir Christopher Wren designed both the church and the pub and two restorations this century have mercifully retained the Watling's character, including its original ceiling beams. Indeed the association with the great architect runs deep, as Wren is reputed to have stayed here while watching work progress on his most famous creation, St Paul's Cathedral.

Food includes bangers, burgers and, presumably to tempt the palates of American tourists, a chicken Caesar salad. There's a varied choice for vegetarians with pasta served with Gorgonzola and pesto, Greek salad with feta cheese and a sandwich of garlic mushrooms and mozzarella.

...also worth trying

The Black Friar

174 Queen Victoria Street (Blackfriars tube and railway)
A beautiful and unique wedge-shaped Art Nouveau pub, originally built in 1903. Real ales usually include Adnams or Brakspear. Despite the crowds, it's still well worth a visit.

WC1

The Lamb

94 Lambs Conduit Street, Bloomsbury

Open: Monday-Saturday: 11-11; Sunday: 12-4 and 7-10.30
Food: Monday-Saturday: 12-2.30 and 6-9; Sunday: 12-2.30
❀ ☎
☎ 020 7405 0713
Russell Square tube
Beers: *Young's Bitter, Special, Triple A all available regularly. Guests include Young's Winter Warmer.*

Even on a rainy Tuesday night in November, there was standing room only at this most beautiful and atmospheric of Bloomsbury pubs.

Built in approximately 1729, the Lamb is famous for being one of only two pubs in the capital to have genuine Victorian snob screens above the horseshoe bar. Made of engraved glass, they were originally installed in many 19th century taverns to allow the upper classes in the saloon to spy on who might be drinking in the public bar, closing shut if they didn't want to be observed by their social inferiors.

Thankfully the pub has no fruit machines or piped music, but instead another Victorian original – the working polyphon, a genteel forerunner to the jukebox. The helpful bar staff will set it working for you, in exchange for a small donation to charity.

Comfy leather chairs and benches line the walls, there's a non-smoking small snug with bar stools and a larger seating area towards the rear of the pub on the left, which leads out to a tiny courtyard at the back. In 1890, many of the music hall stars who performed at the nearby Holborn Empire were frequent visitors to the pub and their sepia-tinted photographs are now displayed.

For the hungry, there's, rather appropriately, lamb's liver and bacon with onion gravy and mashed potato, homemade shepherd's pie and celebration 1729 steak and ale pie. Vegetarians are catered for with homemade vegetable curry and spicy bean burgers.

The Museum Tavern

49 Great Russell Street, Bloomsbury

Open: *Monday-Saturday: 11-11;*
Sunday: 12-10.30
Food: *Monday-Saturday: 11-10;*
Sunday: 12-10
✿
☎ 020 7242 8987
Russell Square/Tottenham Court Road
tube and bus number 7
Beers: *Theakston's Best, Old Peculiar,*
Courage Directors, Abbot Ale and
Charles Wells Bombardier.

It's not difficult to work out from the
pub's name that its neighbour might
just be the British Museum.
According to pub legend, Karl Marx
enjoyed a snifter or two here, allegedly breaking one of the Tavern's mirrors.

Dark, wood paneled and almost perpetually busy, the pub almost didn't make it
into this guide, as the first pint of Theakston's Best I was presented with was
undrinkable. Thankfully the barman agreed with my verdict without hesitation,
was deeply apologetic and immediately replaced it with a rather better kept pint
of Abbot Ale. I'm hoping it was a once in a blue moon mistake, but it's best to be
on your guard. Food is standard pub grub and includes fish and chips, pie and
chips, salads and ploughman's lunches.

The Pakenham Arms

1 Pakenham Street

Open: *Monday-Sunday: 9am -1.30 am*
Food: *Monday-Sunday: 9-3 and 6-9*
♿ ✿ 🐕
☎ 020 7837 6933
Russell Square and King's Cross tube
Beers: *Harvey's, Young's and Fuller's London Pride are available regularly. Guest beers*
include Brakspear Bitter and Special, Adnams, O'Hanlons and Arkells.

Being opposite the country's largest postal sorting office, Mount Pleasant, probably explains the Pakenham Arms' eccentric opening hours, as getting that mail
into your postie's delivery sack is a round-the-clock job.

Once a two–bar pub, now it's one large room, with a central bar. When I visited,
perhaps not surprisingly, most of the punters were postal workers, watching the

so-called 'beautiful game', live on TV. As a crowd of football loathing women, we were prepared to heartily dislike this pub on sight, but against all odds, we ended up enjoying our stay. Unlike too many other bars offering live sports coverage, the atmosphere wasn't dominated by the game and the pub was large enough to accommodate all tastes.

The Pakenham is a particularly good find for cask-conditioned devotees. Apparently the pub was a flagship for the real ale revolution in the 70s and it's reassuring to see it's still flying the flag, with a wide and changing list of beers on tap. Open for breakfast, lunch and dinner, food includes steak and mushroom pie, lasagne, tagliatelle carbonara, tuna pasta bake and veggie pasta bake.

The Plough

27 Museum Street

Open: Monday-Saturday: 11-11; Sunday: 12-10.30
Food: Monday-Sunday: 12-7
&. ❀
☎ 020 7636 7964
Holborn or Tottenham Court Road tube. Buses 7, 91, 73, 25 and 8
Beers: Marston's Pedigree, Burton Ale, Adnams Bitter and Young's Bitter are available regularly. Guests may include Morland's Old Speckled Hen, Abbot Ale and Young's Special.

Two minutes walk down a street full of second hand book shops, the Plough is a quieter – and less expensive – place to adjourn for a drink, after an hour or two spent wandering in the British Museum, than its neighbour, the Museum Tavern. Small and traditionally decorated, one glance at the menu and you know you're at the centre of London's tourist trail, as meals like fish and chips, steak and kidney pie and vegetarian quiche are also translated into French and Spanish.

Princess Louise

208-209 High Holborn

Open: Monday-Friday: 11-11; Saturday: 12-11; Sunday: closed
Food: Monday-Saturday: 12-3 and 5.30-9
☎ 020 7405 8816
Holborn tube
Beers: Samuel Smith Old Brewery Bitter

The Princess Louise is a splendidly preserved grand old dame, offering one of the finest examples of Victorian pub architecture in the capital.

Originally built in 1872 and now a Grade II listed building, today's interior dates back to 1891 and includes marble, etched windows, enormous engraved and gilt mirrors, Portland stone columns, an ornate crimson and gold ceiling and a vast central bar. Not that I could be expected to vouch at first hand for this, but the Gents' loo is rumoured to be particularly palatial and subject to a protection order in its own right.

A free house until relatively recently, now the pub is owned by Sam Smith's brewery. Mercifully, it's escaped their capital keg blitz and still serves the hand pumped stuff "just like you get it up north", according to one CAMRA member who recommended the pub for inclusion in this guide. Food includes fish and chips, bangers and mash, roast chicken, spinach and ricotta cannelloni and vegetable kiev.

The Swan

7 Cosmo Place

Open: *Monday-Saturday: 11-11; Sunday: 12-10.30*
Food: *Monday-Saturday: 11-11; Sunday: 12-10.30*
& ☎
☎ *020 7837 6223*
Russell Square or Holborn tube. Buses 68, 168 and 91
Beers: *Theakston's Best and Old Peculiar, Greene King IPA and Abbot Ale and Courage Directors are available regularly. There are always one or two guests, that might include Everard's Tiger, Charles Wells Bombardier and Gale's HSB.*

Although it's slap bang in the middle of an area with a largely transient population of tourists, somehow the Swan manages to feel as friendly, warm and welcoming as a street corner local, providing a relatively calm and comfortable place to idle away an hour or two.

While it may not offer much in the way of history or interesting architecture, this wood panelled and stripped floorboards pub is tucked away in a pleasant pedestrian side street, a couple of minutes from Great Ormond Street children's hospital.

Under the careful scrutiny of the publican, the Swan is developing a good reputation for the quality of its real ale, reflected in its inclusion in CAMRA's *Good Beer Guide* 2001. Food is served in healthy portions and might include cod and chips, giant Yorkshire puddings filled with beef, sausages or mushrooms, mash and onion gravy, and all in one pies, featuring beef and ale, chicken and ham or lamb and rosemary. Vegetarian choices include spicy bean burgers and red pepper lasagne.

Three Cups

21-22 Sandland Street, Bloomsbury

Open: Monday-Friday: 11-11; Sat and Sunday: closed
Food: Monday-Friday: 12-2.30
&

☎ *020 831 4302*
Chancery Lane or Holborn tube. Buses 8, 25, 242 and 501
Beers: Young's Bitter, Special and Triple A.

Five minutes walk from Lincoln's Inn Fields, this busy one bar pub, with its Victorian exterior, is set at the front of an old coaching yard. Open during weekdays only, this Young's pub attracts a mixed, convivial crowd of drinkers. Food includes scampi, Cumberland sausages, homemade shepherd's pie, three cheese pasta and broccoli bake and cheese paninis.

also worth trying...

Cittie of Yorke

22 High Holborn (Chancery Lane tube)
Enormous old baronial hall style pub — with a vaulted roof, the longest bar in London, cubicles and massive vats — that is popular with tourists, law students and the legal profession. On tap is Sam Smith's Old Brewery Bitter.

Queen's Larder

1 Queen Square (Russell Square tube)
Lovely, tiny, atmospheric, Grade II listed pub that gets its name from the time when Queen Charlotte allegedly rented the pub's cellar to store delicacies for her husband, King George III, who was recuperating nearby from one of his regular bouts of 'madness'. Beers include Flowers IPA and Wadworth's 6X.

WC2

Chandos

27 St Martins Lane

Open: Monday-Saturday: 11-11; Sunday: 12-10.30
Food: Monday-Saturday: 11-6; Sunday: 12-6
🛆, *but upstairs only until 7pm*
☎ *020 7836 1401*
Charing Cross tube and railway plus buses that run to Trafalgar Square
Beers: Samuel Smith Old Brewery Bitter

Almost opposite Trafalgar Square and a few minutes walk from the National Gallery, the National Portrait Gallery and the English National Opera, the Chandos provides an ideal meeting point.

The drawback to its prime location is that it's almost always heaving with tourists, office workers and theatre-goers – good for Sam Smith's brewery who own it, but not quite so good for you, if you're attempting to find your friends here. The secret is to arrange where you're going to stand – forget sitting – and stay there, or you're all likely to spend your evening walking around in circles.

The bar downstairs has wood panelling, a few tiles and loud music, while upstairs is a bit quieter. Incidentally, the name comes from Lord Chandos, who was a patron of the German composer, Handel.

Food includes chicken with honey and ginger, tortellini stuffed with cheese and a mushroom sauce and walnut, leek and Wensleydale flan.

George IV

28 Portugal Street

Open: Monday-Friday: 11-11; closed Saturday and Sunday
Food: Monday-Friday: 11-3 and 5-9
☎ *020 7831 3221*
Holborn tube
Beers: Fuller's London Pride and Bass

Close to the London School of Economics, the George caters for students desperate to avoid their studies by providing an upstairs games room, complete with pool table, giant Connect4 and Jenja.

There's a lot of dark wood, an open fire and tall tables surrounded by high stools, rather than cosy alcoves and padded seats. Entertainment includes a pub quiz every fortnight and karaoke every month. Food includes Thai vegetable curry, Cajun chicken baguette and steak pie.

Lamb and Flag

33 Rose Street

Open: Monday to Thursday: 11-11; Friday and Saturday: 11-10.45; Sunday: 12-10.30
Food: Monday-Saturday: 11-3; Sunday: 12-3
☎, but lunchtimes only
☎ 020 7497 9504
Covent Garden and Charing Cross tube
Beers: Courage Best and Directors, Young's Bitter and Special, Marston's Pedigree and Tetley's are all available regularly. Guests include Morland's Old Speckled Hen, Burton Ale and Young's Triple A.

Licensed since the reign of Elizabeth I, the Lamb and Flag is the oldest tavern in Covent Garden.

According to documents of the time, Rose Street in the 17th century had a rather shabby reputation compared to its modern-day incarnation, with houses 'fit only for mechanics and persons of mean quality'. Tell that to the affluent and beautiful people who strut the streets of Covent Garden and would probably sell their granny to live here.

Previously called the Cooper's Arms, its present name dates from 1833. Colloquially it was also known as the Bucket of Blood, as bare-knuckle prize fights were once staged in the upstairs room. Called the Dryden room, it's named in honour of the poet John Dryden who was attacked and almost killed in the alleyway, by a gang of thugs hired by the mistress of King Charles II. Thankfully today the room is used for the infinitely more civilised pursuit of listening to jazz on Sunday evenings – entrance is free.

Food is also served upstairs and includes traditional roasts, fish and chips, jacket potatoes and macaroni cheese.

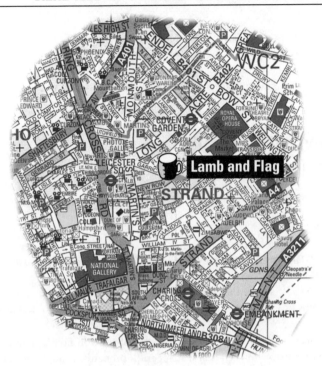

The Marquess of Anglesey

39 Bow Street

Open: Monday-Saturday: 11-11;
Sunday: 12-10.30
Food: Monday-Saturday: 12-10;
Sunday: 12-8
☺
☎ *020 7240 3216*
Covent Garden tube
Beers: Young's Bitter, Special, Triple
A are available regularly. Winter
Warmer is seasonally available from
October to March.

This lively, bustling Young's pub,
near to the Royal Opera House,
attracts a mixed crowd that might
include musicians and others who
earn their living in the nearby
theatres.

Built in the 1950s but furnished in contemporary style, there are two bars and the upstairs one leads to a small raised restaurant area at the back. Food offers some imaginative vegetarian options, such as goat's cheese salad and filo parcel with spinach and cottage cheese. Other choices include fish and chips, pies and various sandwiches.

The Marquis of Granby

51-52 Chandos Place

Open: Monday-Saturday: 12-11; Sunday: 12-10.30
Food: Monday-Sunday: 12-5
& ☎ *until 6pm*
☎ *020 7836 7657*
Charing Cross, Leicester Square and Covent Garden tube
Beers: Adnams, Fuller's London Pride and Timothy Taylor's Landlord are available regularly. There are various guests.

Tucked down a side street, the Marquis can be a slightly less frantic spot to enjoy a well-kept pint or two than other pubs that share its proximity to Trafalgar Square.

The small, cheese-shaped Victorian style bar has a cast iron fireplace, leaded glass and wood partitions at both ends and stripped floorboards throughout. There's also an upstairs room. Food includes the usual fish and chips, sausage and mash and vegetable lasagne and there's often a homemade soup.

The Opera Tavern

23 Catherine Street

Open: Monday-Saturday: 12-11;
Sunday: 12-8
Food: Monday-Saturday: 12-3 and
5-8
&
☎ *020 7379 9832*
Covent Garden tube
Beers: Adnams, Greene King IPA and Bass are available regularly. Guests include Wadworth's 6X, Adnams Broadside, Burton Ale and Tetley.

Most of the time, I can endure the dubious delights of sports coverage on television, but every now and then I want to

scream 'turn it off!' – and visiting the Opera Tavern provided one of those rare moments.

From the outside, the pub has a wonderful Victorian façade, featuring beautiful windows enhanced by glorious floral displays in the summer. It was built in 1879 by the architect Jonathan Treacher, who specialised in pub design. Inside there's wooden paneling, etched mirrors and a plethora of colourful posters and photographs of the many stars who've trodden the boards at its opposite neighbour, the Theatre Royal Drury Lane. Charles II is said to have used a nearby secret passageway beneath the road, when he wanted to meet his favourite mistress, Nell Gwynn, at the theatre.

With all this splendour, is there any need to have televisions positioned at both ends of the bar, blaring out the football results? Perhaps we should have known better than to arrive at something to 5 on a Saturday afternoon, but given there's a 'sports bar' upstairs, complete with pool table, can't the tellies be moved there, allowing the rest of us to enjoy what the landlord boasts is a 'friendly village atmosphere' in peace?

Despite this downside, it's still the haunt of luvvies aplenty and, according to the publican, is a good place to pick up an autograph. It's also the very real haunt of ghost Robert Baddeley, an actor who died in 1794. If only he could be trained to use the remote control...

The Porterhouse

21-22 Maiden Lane

Open: *Monday-Saturday: 11-11; Sunday: 12-10.30*
Food: *Monday-Saturday: 12-9; Sunday: 12-5*
♿ ⚘

☏ *020 7379 7917*

Covent Garden, Leicester Square and Charing Cross tube
Beers: TSB and various porters. There is also a wide range of bottled beers.

Bottles, bottles everywhere and lots and lots to drink. A hymn to the dark stuff, the beers at the Porterhouse are brewed in Dublin, using no chemicals, and are unpasteurised.

TSB is especially brewed for the Covent Garden bar and is 'a traditional style pale ale with a modern interpretation' but we cut straight to the chase, trying Plain Porter and Oyster Stout. Both are award-winners, but I particularly liked the latter, which was thick, creamy, chocolatey and very moreish. A whim that's easy to satisfy, as the helpful bar staff seem able to spot an emptying glass at 20 paces and home in, asking if you'd like a refill.

Described by the patrons as 'Victorian industrial chic', whatever that might mean, the bar is multi-levelled and there is copper piping everywhere. The music is loud and gets louder, particularly from Wednesday through to Sunday, when there are live bands and DJs.

Every wall features a glass cabinet full of different bottles of beers from all over the world, making it the equivalent of a jeweller's shop window for beer aficionados. Indeed, they're trying to create the world's largest bottle collection and if you manage to find one they don't already have, take it along and they'll exchange it for a free pint – at their prices, that's not a bad offer.

Food includes whacky delights like Thai Irish stew – lamb and sweet potato, sealed with lime and Thai spices and finished with a coconut sauce, served with a wedge of soda bread. Continuing the oyster theme, there's also oyster stout sausages, served with mash and mustard sauce, and a half or a dozen oysters. For veggies, there's pasta with spinach and cream cheese and Thai noodle salad.

The Salisbury

90 St Martins Lane

Open: *Monday-Saturday: 11-11; Sunday: 12-10.30*
Food: *Monday-Saturday: 11-11; Sunday: 12-10.30*
⚘

☏ *020 7836 5863*

Leicester Square and Charing Cross tube
Beers: Theakston's Best and Courage Directors are available regularly. There are occasional guests including Brakspear and Ridley's Rumpus.

If sumptuous, opulent and grand are apt descriptions of what you look for in pub décor and the flamboyant Lawrence Llewelyn Bowen is your favourite interior designer, the Salisbury is for you.

Set in the heart of London's theatre-land, the ornate black and gold frontage opens up to a riot of heavily etched glass, acid etched mirrors covering the whole of one wall, red chandeliers, bare breasted bronze nymph lamps, pillars, brass and a splendid central marble bar. The dark, womb-like atmosphere is enhanced by the curved, red velvet covered seats, hand carved mahogany and dark red plaster-work ceiling.

Marianne Faithful was photographed here in 1966 for the artwork for her album cover, *Come my Way*. Renamed as the Shaftsbury, the pub also featured in the 1960s Dirk Bogarde film, *Victim*, the first British film to deal sympathetically with homosexuality. Food includes platters featuring chicken wings, barbeque ribs, crudités, sandwiches and nachos.

Sherlock Holmes

10 Northumberland Avenue

Open: Monday-Saturday: 11-11;
Sunday: 12-10.30
Food: Monday-Sunday: 12-10
♿ ❀ ☎
☎ 020 7930 2644
Charing Cross or Embankment tube
Beers: Morland's Old Speckled Hen, Wadworth 6X, Flowers IPA, Boddingtons, Fuller's London Pride and Adnams are all available regularly. Guests include Caledonian Deuchars IPA.

It doesn't take a top-notch detective to deduce that this

pub has a 'theme', but thankfully, unlike most of its modern-day counterparts, it's done so well that it serves as a tourist attraction in its own right.

Boasting 'the most authentic Baker Street study in the world' – which is also the pub's dining room – the walls are covered with unique memorabilia featuring Sherlock Holmes and his creator, Sir Arthur Conan Doyle. The mementos include old film and television stills of the actors who have played the great detective, theatre bills advertising the stage adaptations of the tales, extracts from the novels themselves and even a mock head of a Baskerville hound.

There's a fine selection of ales and food includes shepherd's pie, bangers and mash, steak and mushroom in ale pie and Stilton and cheddar stuffed mushrooms.

East London

E1

Dickens Inn

St Katherine's Way

Open: *Monday-Saturday: 11-11; Sunday: 12-10.30*
Food: *Monday-Friday: 12-3; Sat and Sunday: 12-5*
& ✿
☎ *020 7488 2208*
Tower Hill or London Bridge tube
Beers: *Courage Best, Courage Directors, Morland's Old Speckled Hen and Theakston's Old Peculiar are available regularly, while guests might include Theakston's XB and Charles Wells Bombardier.*

Once an old spice warehouse dating from the 18th century, this large imposing building was converted to a ground-floor pub, complete with restaurants on the first and second floors, in 1976.

Today it's a tourist magnet, set on the harbour side amongst the pretty affluence of St Katharine's Dock and barely a stone's throw from Tower Bridge and the Tower of London. With its European Redwood beams and pillars and window box bedecked balconies, from the outside the Dickens Inn looks like an attractive prospect for wiling away an hour or two.

Unfortunately, we discovered that the packaging proved to be much more alluring than the contents. Once inside, the music was far too loud and of the Spice Girls variety; the service was sloppy – we looked at the remains of someone's dinner for the 45 minutes we sat down – and, as a result, the promised atmosphere sadly lacking. On the other hand, our beers were well kept, if pricey, and the views are delightful. At one point, there was a few minutes blissful silence between Mel B's warbling and Rocking Around the Christmas Tree with someone or another, and it was possible to see that the whole experience would be vastly improved if someone simply located the off switch on the sound system. I assume that's what happens during the quiz night held during the winter months.

Visitors to the Dickens would find it hard to go hungry. The first floor restaurant serves pizza while the à la carte offers traditionally British – and more expensive – food. In contrast, the pub sticks to stalwarts like fish and chips, chilli con carne and sausage and mash. Vegetarian options include spinach and ricotta cannelloni and stir fried vegetables in filo pastry with a pimento coulis.

Good Samaritan

87 Turner Street

Open: Monday-Saturday: 11-11; Sunday:
12-10.30
Food: All day, everyday
&. ☎, until 8pm
☎ 020 7247 9146
Whitechapel tube
Beers: Regulars are Courage Directors and
Theakston's SB while guest or seasonal
ales might include Marston's Pedigree or
beers brewed by Young's or Wychwood.
Also stocks St Peter's Golden and Wheat
bottled beers.

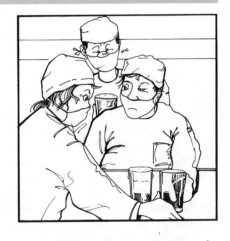

If you're planning to fall suddenly ill,
there's probably no better place to do
it than here, as eight out of 10 of the Good Samaritan's customers are connected
to the medical profession, many of them doctors, and the pub sits amidst the various departments of the Royal London Hospital.

Rebuilt in 1937, the landlord believes that the Good Samaritan is probably the
best pub in Whitechapel and I, for one, would find it hard to argue with his view.
Only the churlish might point out there's not a lot in the way of competition.
With its Victorian parlour-style lounge, cosy seating, open fireplaces and old black
and white photographs on the walls, it's an undemanding place to relax and
unwind over a pint or two. And if you're working in today's National Health
Service, you've earned a drink.

Food is served all day and includes giant Yorkshire puddings served with sausage
and mash or beef and vegetables, curries, baked potatoes, roast red pepper lasagne
and mushroom pepper pot. A real find.

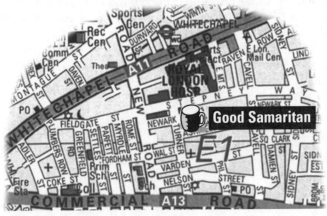

London Hospital Tavern Urban Bar

176 Whitechapel Road

Open: *Monday-Friday: 12-12; Saturday: 12-1am; Sunday: 12-10.30*
Food: *All day, everyday*
♿
☎ *020 7247 7659*
Whitechapel tube; buses 25 and N25
Beers: *Adnams, Fuller's London Pride, Morland's Old Speckled Hen, Greene King IPA*

The London Hospital Tavern has undergone a metamorphosis, or should I say shed a skin, since it added Urban Bar to its name. Where once there were pictures on the ceiling and wooden alcoves, now there are live snakes and lizards – but don't panic, they're not the lounge variety but safely locked away in tanks. There's also a tiger-striped exterior, wacky lighting and discrete indie music. The overall effect is as far away from a traditional English pub as you can get and more in keeping with a trendy Parisian bar – or at least Camden High Street.

You either love it or hate it and our group was three to one in favour. Despite the cool décor, staff are warmly welcoming and no sooner had we sat down than a free bowl of popcorn was plonked on the table, while our barman went out of his way to tempt the pregnant member of our party with a range of unusual soft drinks. Apparently the staff also introduce tables of customers to each other, so it could be a good venue for the single and fancy free or those bored with their own social circle and looking for a new one.

As well as the infinitely better than average taped offerings, there's live music every Tuesday and Sunday and late night opening every day except the Sabbath. Food is a little disappointing, hailing from the ubiquitous steak and ale pie, chilli con carne and vegetarian lasagne school of pub fodder, but it's served all day and every day.

And although it's a long way from the traditional English beach huts and fancy tea rooms of Southwold to the bright street markets and multi-ethnicity of Whitechapel, the London Hospital Tavern produced as good a pint of Adnams as I've supped anywhere.

Let's face it, if real ale is to begin to tempt the palates of the under-30s, and so have a future, this is precisely the kind of trendy bar it needs to be selling in. Bravo – but lose the reptiles...

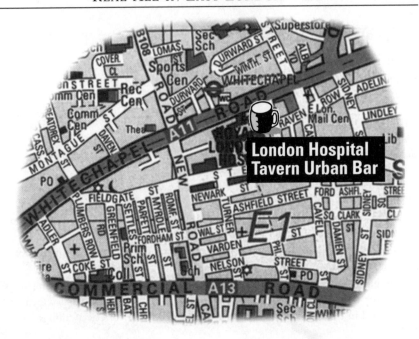

London Hospital
Tavern Urban Bar

Princess of Prussia

15 Prescot Street

Open: Monday-Friday: 11-11; closed Saturday and Sunday
Food: Monday-Friday: all day
& ❀ ☎ *during the day*
☎ *020 7480 5304*
Aldgate East and Tower tube, plus Docklands Light Railway
Beers: Courage Directors and Theakstons. The publican plans to have guest ales in the near future.

Next door to the famous Indian restaurant, Café Spice Namaste, the Princess of Prussia is described by the enthusiastic landlord as a "no frills and no plastic, typical friendly local pub but without the locals, as office workers are our bread and butter".

With the Tower of London just eight minutes walk away, the pub is, dare I say it, at the heart of Jack the Ripper country, with the restaurant next door once functioning as the courtroom that issued the warrant for his arrest.

Food is a cut above the average pub grub and includes Cajun sausage and chilli mash, chicken carbonara and Aberdeen Angus beef lasagne. The options for vegetarians change daily and there are always veggie burgers and a ploughman's.

The White Swan

21 Alie Street

Open: Monday-Friday: 11-11; Saturday: 12-11; closed on Sunday
Food: Monday-Friday: 12-3
&

☎ *020 7702 0448*
Aldgate and Aldgate East; buses 15, 25, 115, 215
Beers: *Shepherd Neame beers including Spitfire, Bishop's Finger and Masterbrew. Seasonal ales include Early Bird and Goldings.*

This 19th century traditional Shepherd Neame owned pub, on the edge of the City and within five minutes stroll of the Tower of London, comes highly applauded by CAMRA members for the outstanding quality of its ale. As one put it: "The beer is first class and I make it a point to stop off here for a pint after I've been to Lloyds, as it removes the bad taste from my mouth!" Recommendation indeed.

The publican hosts a quiz night once a month between different local companies and there's a pool table and darts board. Food choices include an all-day breakfast, a 10oz cod in batter, omelettes and speciality rolls with a variety of fillings.

...also worth trying

Pride of Spitalfields

3 Heneage Street (Aldgate East tube)
Small, lively, single bar back street Fuller's pub with a mixed clientele, featuring photographs of old East End scenes, old bottles and chamber pots. It's a handy watering hole before or after a curry in nearby Brick Lane.

The Prospect of Whitby

57 Wapping Wall (Wapping tube)
Originally built in 1520, the Prospect was once the regular haunt of the infamous and bloodthirsty Hanging Judge Jeffries, who came here to gloat at the sight of men he had ordered to be executed, hanging from gallows across the river. Today, it's a beautifully preserved and atmospheric, gas lamp lit, historic riverside pub that is almost always choc-a-bloc. Although it's firmly on the tourist trail, it's still worth a glimpse.

Town of Ramsgate

62 Wapping High Street (Tower Hill or Wapping tube)
Taking its name from the Ramsgate fishermen, who used to land their catch at Wapping Old Steps, this is a proper pub, full of regulars. It features an eye-catching etched glass depiction of Ramsgate Harbour at the front of the pub's long and thin bar, friendly bar staff and a well-kept pint of Fuller's London Pride.

E2

The Approach Tavern

47 Approach Road, Bethnal Green

Open: Monday: 5-11; Tuesday to Saturday: 12-11 and Sunday: 12-10.30
Food: Tue-Saturday: 12-3 and 7-10; Sunday: 1-5
 ♿ ❊ ☃
☏ *020 8980 2321*
Bethnal Green or Mile End tube and buses 106 and 253
Beers: Regulars include Marston's Pedigree, Young's Special, Fuller's London Pride and Adnams. Guest ales might include Greene King IPA, Fuller's ESB and Timothy Taylor's Landlord.

With an art gallery on the first floor, the Approach attracts as varied a bunch of regulars as you're likely to find anywhere – "everyone from brain surgeons to road sweepers" says publican Julian Apperley.

Held in high regard by all who frequent it, this traditional Victorian corner local boasts a warm and genuinely welcoming atmosphere, enhanced by dark wood floors and walls. There's a wide range of beers, including a changing guest list, and food includes steak, curries, vegetarian options and a roast on Sundays.

There's a pub quiz on Tuesdays. It's also a handy watering hole after a visit to the nearby Museum of Childhood on Cambridge Heath Road.

E3

Bow Bells

116 Bow Road

Open: *Monday-Saturday: 11-11; Sunday: 12-10.30*
Food: *Monday-Friday: 11-3; Sunday: 12-4*

&

☎ *020 8981 7317*

Bow Road tube; Bow Church Docklands Light Railway and buses 25, 8 and D8
Beers: Fuller's London Pride, Adnams Bitter and Burton Ale are regularly available.
Guest beers include Brakspear Bitter, Morland's Old Speckled Hen, Young's and
Kimberley

The Bow Bells pub benefits from the mistaken assumption that the church over the road is the one immortalised in the nursery rhyme. Usually tourists only discover that they've got it wrong when they nip into the pub for a quick drink after their sightseeing.

But, with its listed Victorian façade and hospitable surroundings, there are many less pleasant places you could wind up spending an hour or two. A busy locals' pub, there's a quiz every Wednesday, a disco on Fridays and either live music or a disco on Saturday night. Food includes steak, chips and salad, fish and chips and jacket potatoes and there are vegetarian options like Quorn burgers and lasagne. And watch out for the resident ghost – the pub used to be on a "haunted London" mystery tour. Apparently one of its favourite, if bizarre tricks is to flush the loo in the ladies' toilets. It takes all sorts.

Coborn Arms

8 Coborn Road

Open: *Monday-Saturday: 11-11; Sunday: 12-10.30*
Food: *Monday-Friday: 12-2.30 and 6-10; Sat and Sunday: 1-9*

& ✿

☎ *020 8980 3793*

Mile End tube and bus 25
Beers: Young's Bitter, Special and Triple A. Guests and seasonal brews include Young's
Winter Warmer. Bottled conditioned beers include Young's Special London Ale.

This traditional, comfortable Young's pub, decorated with old photographs and maps, is popular with locals for the high standard of its food and the quality of its beer – it makes a regular appearance in CAMRA's *Good Beer Guide*.

Food options include steak and mushroom in Young's ale pie, bangers and mash with the unusual addition of deep fried parsnips and supreme of salmon. Vegetarian choices have a Mediterranean feel, with roasted vegetable and tomato pie and baked aubergine, stuffed with peppers, tomato, courgette and mushrooms.

The Crown

223 Grove Road

Open: M: 5-11; Tuesday-Saturday: 10.30-11 Sunday: 10.30-10.30
Food: M: 6.30-10.30; Tuesday to Saturday: 10.30-3 and 6.30-10; Sunday: 10.30-3.30 and 6.30-10
& ❀ ⛌
☎ 020 8981 9998
Mile End tube and bus 277
Beers: All are organic and include: Singhboulton, brewed by Pitfield, Caledonian Golden Promise and St Peter's Organic Ale. Guest beers include Pitfield's Eco Warrior and Black Eagle. There's a range of bottle conditioned organic beers too, including Riedenburger Weisse and Sam Smith's.

A decade or even five years ago, if anyone had suggested that barely 10 minutes walk from Mile End, there would be a completely organic pub, I would have been hardly able to contain my laughter. That anyone seriously thought that the East End of London, famous for its old-style mobster connections and dodgy dealing, could support an eco-friendly, ethically conscious pub, rather than one sporting bullet holes in the walls, would have been cause enough to send for the men in white coats. But I'm pleased to say that the last laugh is on me, because the Crown opened for business in the summer of 2000 and was quickly a huge success.

The sister pub of the Duke of Cambridge in Islington, the Crown is only the second pub in the country to be certified by the Soil Association to serve a huge range of organic beer, wine and food. Run by the innovative and pioneering partnership of Geetie Singh and Esther Boulton, the pub is ideally situated overlooking Victoria Park and, rather fittingly, near to Mile End Regeneration Park. Originally built in 1862, it's a listed building and has been lovingly restored by the new owners, who have taken great pains to preserve as many original features as possible, including its name. Décor is minimalist, complete with mismatched chairs and tables and stripped floors. There are no smoking dining rooms on the first floor, which offer waiter service, but the menu is exactly the same as the downstairs pub. Children are not just tolerated, they're positively welcomed, and there's no need to leave the family mutt at home either, as dogs' water bowls are thoughtfully dotted around the ground floor bar. As befits the style, there are no gaming machines, music or any entertainment other than the buzz of proper conversation.

The range of beers is interesting and the food, although not cheap, is stunning. The menu changes daily and might include rib eye steak, chips and Caesar salad, grilled tuna with pepperonata and spinach or chicken liver paté with pear chutney, pickles and toast. Vegetarians can choose from two options – perhaps pumpkin and roast pepper risotto or bruschetta with grilled vegetables, goats cheese and pesto. All are available in child-sized portions. As an East Ender might sum up, it's a diamond boozer.

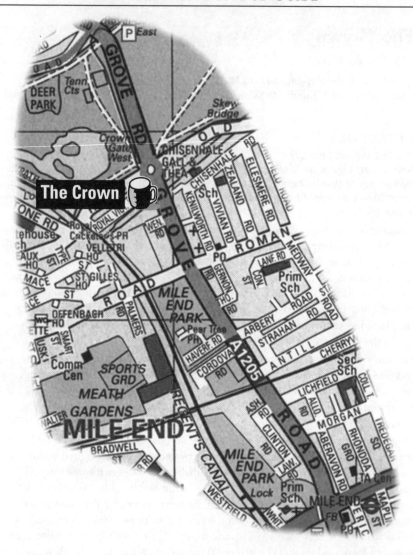

E4

The Royal Oak

219 Kings Head Hill, Chingford

Open: Monday-Saturday: 11-11 Sunday: 12-10.30
Food: Monday-Saturday: 12-2.30 and 7-9, except Monday evening, when there is no food; Sunday: 12.30-2.30
& ❀ ➳ Ⓟ
☎ 020 8529 1492
Chingford railway station and bus 313
Beers: Courage Directors and beers from the McMullen range, including AK, Country, Gladstone and Special Reserve.

In an area poorly served by pubs, perhaps not surprisingly this spacious, traditional two bar McMullen's pub has a strong local following.

Entertainment includes a pub quiz on alternate Sundays and there's a patio and separate dining room. Food options include steak and ale or chicken and ham pie, lasagne, vegetable crumble or spinach and feta cheese goujons.

E5

Anchor and Hope

15 High Hill Ferry, Clapton

Open: Monday-Saturday: 11-3 and 5.30-11; Sunday: 12-10.30
Food: None
& ❀ ➳
☎ 020 8806 1730
Clapton railway
Beers: Fuller's ESB and London Pride are regularly available.

Sitting on the banks of the River Lea, facing Walthamstow Marshes, the Anchor and Hope makes regular appearances in CAMRA's *Good Beer Guide*. Indeed, this very popular and often packed pub won the local CAMRA Pub of the Year award in 1999. It's a well-deserved reward for landlord Leslie Heath, who has been pulling pints in this tiny no frills local for a half-century. Note that there's no food, but the view and a well-kept, reasonably priced pint of Fuller's should help to keep any hunger pangs at bay.

Princess of Wales

146 Lea Bridge Road

Open: *Monday-Saturday: 11-11; Sunday: 12-10.30*
Food: *Monday-Saturday: 12-3 and 6-8.30; Sunday: 12-4*
&. ❀ ℗
☎ *020 8533 3463*
Clapton railway and buses 48 and 56
Beers: *The Young's range of beers including Bitter, Special, Triple A. Guests include Winter Warmer.*

Set back from the road and overlooking the River Lea, the Princess of Wales is a pleasant place to enjoy a pint of Young's beer, particularly in the summer, when you can sit outside and watch the herons catch their supper. For humans, food is the standard cod, chicken barbeque or steak, all served with chips and there are veggie burgers and lasagne for vegetarians.

E8

Dove Freehouse and Kitchen

24-26 Broadway Market

Open: *Monday to Thursday: 12-11; Friday and Saturday: 12-12; Sunday: 12-10.30*
Food: *Monday to Thursday: 12-3 and 6-10; Friday and Saturday: 12-10.30; Sunday: 12-10*
&. *but limited toilet facilities;* ❀ ⚑ *but no nappy changing facilities*
☎ *020 7275 7617*
Bethnal Green tube or London Fields railway
Beers: *Flowers IPA, Boddingtons, Marston's Pedigree, Morland's Old Speckled Hen and one guest beer. Specialises in Belgian beers, those on draft including Hoegaarden, Leffe Blond, Leffe Brun, Bellevue Kriek, Bellevue Gueuze and De Koninck. There's a huge range of bottled beers including trappist and abbey ales, fruit beers and regional beers.*

Don't want to find yourself rubbing shoulders with unreconstructed comedians of the Bernard Manning school of stand-up? Well the Dove Freehouse and Kitchen is the pub for you, as publican Elizabeth Grogan was the first in London to ban all sexist, racist and homophobic references from her premises.

Multi award-winning, the Dove offers a warm welcome for everyone, good food and an excellent choice of home grown and Belgian beers. There are board games rather than beeping quiz machines and relaxed background music instead of a thumping base line.

Food is classy and deemed worthy of a star in Susan Nowak's CAMRA guide, *Good Pub Food*. The menu changes daily and might include whole roast trout, boeuf bourguignon, mussels, three cheese lasagne and roast butternut pumpkin.

There are also five kinds of meat sausages made especially for the pub and incorporating Belgian beer, plus one non-meat variety.

While on the outside it may look like a traditional tavern, the décor has been described by one critic as "more like the set of a David Lynch movie than a pub". So why not go along and judge for yourself whether the combination of a cosy fire and fake leopard skin transports you to Twin Peaks.

Pub on the Park

19 Martello Street, London Fields

Open: Monday-Saturday: 11-11; Sunday: 12-10.30
Food: Monday-Saturday: 12-4; Sunday: 12-6
&, ❀ ⛾ *substantial unmetered parking available*
☎ 020 7275 9586
Bethnal Green tube, London Fields railway and buses 55 and 253
Beers: a changing menu of real ales, which might include Fuller's London Pride and some of their seasonal ales and O'Hanlons seasonal beers.

I have a soft spot, if not a debt of gratitude, to this free house as it helped to keep me relatively sane and cheerful when I did a two-year stint working in beleaguered Hackney Council's press office several years ago.

Back then, it was called Taylors and customers were a diverse bunch of dispirited Council workers in need of a pick-me-up, various political factions trying to sell each other their ideologies via a newspaper and cricket fans – the pub has two teams. More than a decade later, all that seems to have changed are Hackney's house prices and the pub's name.

Sitting smack in the middle of London Fields – a pleasant stretch of green in an otherwise urban sprawl – the pub really comes into its own when the weather heats up, with an outdoor decking area that seats 200 people. As proprietors Ann and Brendan McDonald proudly brag, it's the largest beer garden in London. During the summer months there's live music outside and there's a Council-managed children's playground within 50 yards. If cricket's not to your liking, petanque is also played here.

The pub sports a green and gold exterior and if you're forced inside, you'll find a pleasant interior with large windows, lots of pot plants and stripped floors. Food includes interesting baguettes, like chicken and yoghurt with mint, honey and mustard glazed ham and the full array of Sunday roasts, including a vegetarian option. Non-meat eaters could also choose lentil Wellington or spinach and mushroom lasagne. Well worth a visit.

Railway Tavern

339 Mare Street

Open: Monday-Saturday: 11-11; Sunday: 12-10.30
Food: Monday-Saturday: 12-3; Sunday: 12.30-4
& ⛾ *until 7pm*
☎ 020 8985 4184
Hackney Central railway and buses 30, 38, 106, 253, 48, 55, 276, W15, 52, D6 and 242
Beers: Charles Wells Bombardier and guests include Discovery Golden Ale, Summer Solstice, Festival Gold, Lock, Stock and Barrel, Josephine Gambleys and Noggin.

This Charles Wells pub in the heart of Hackney offers a traditional East End welcome, including free jellied eels, cockles and winkles on Sundays, and a cheap pint to boot, with all real ales priced at £1.70.

Close to the historic and beautifully restored Hackney Empire – which provides an eclectic mix of alternative comedy nights, theatre, pantomime and other special events – the Railway is ideal for a pre-theatre drink. Or you could choose to stay put and enjoy the live music at weekends.

There's a comprehensive menu, featuring steak sandwiches, meat and vegetable lasagnes and what the publican describes as "the best BLT in London". Note that a cask breather is often used.

E10

King William IV

816 High Road, Leyton

Open: Monday-Saturday: 11-11; Sunday: 12-10.30
Food: Monday-Saturday: 12-3 and 5.30-8.30; Sunday: 12.30-5
 ♿ ❀ 🍽 *until 7pm*
☎ *020 8556 2460*

Walthamstow tube and railway; Leyton tube and railway and buses 69 and 97
Beers: Fuller's ESB and London Pride and Woodforde's Wherry. The pub has its own micro brewery on site, producing regular beers, like Just William and William the Conqueror, and seasonal options.

Such is the commitment of the King William IV to the cause of cask conditioned ale, that they installed their very own micro brewery in a converted stable block in November 2000.

Now up-and-running, the five barrel brewery produces a 3.8 ABV session beer, called Just William, the slightly stronger William the Conqueror at 4.4 and one changing seasonal brew – for example, in December they produced a spiced winter warmer. The ales have gone down a treat with locals and other pubs have given a thumbs up by placing orders.

A large, traditionally decorated East End free house, the King William IV offers a relaxed atmosphere that remains unhindered by a jukebox or pool tables but, for those in need of entertainment, there's a pub quiz on Sunday evenings.

Food is of the same high standard as the beer and includes various homemade specialities for meat-eaters and vegetarians alike. You might choose from lamb burgers, steak and ale pie, a galette of oven roasted vegetables, pasta puttanesca, vegetable cannelloni or various freshly baked baguettes.

E11

Birkbeck Tavern

45 Langthorne Road, Leytonstone

Open: Monday-Saturday: 11-11; Sunday: 12-10.30
Food: Monday-Saturday: 12-3
&. ❀
☎ 020 8539 2584
Leyton tube
Beers: Courage Best, Bass, Fuller's London Pride and Marston's Pedigree and there are at least four guest beers each week.

What more could any real ale lover wish for than a publican who replies "too many to list" when asked which guest beers they might serve during a year? In addition to offering at least four guest ales each week, this no frills Victorian two-bar pub, set in a back street near to Leyton tube station, also plans to hold mini beer festivals throughout the year. Food is a variety of sandwiches.

The Duke of Edinburgh

79 Nightingale Lane, Wanstead

Open: Monday-Saturday: 11-11; Sunday: 12-10.30
Food: Monday-Friday: 12-7; Saturday: 12-3
&. ❀ ℗
☎ 020 8989 0014
Wanstead or Snaresbrook tube; bus W12
Beers: Young's, Adnams and a guest ale that is changed monthly.

This attractive 100 year-old one bar local must be one of the few pubs left in the capital that boasts a shove ha'penny board. Other entertainment includes bar billiards, darts and a longstanding quiz evening, held every Monday. Food options feature home made steak pie, shepherd's pie or honey roast ham, while vegetarians might choose three cheese pasta with broccoli or a variety of omelettes.

E13

The Black Lion

59-61 High Street, Plaistow

Open: *Monday to Thursday: 11-3, 5-11; Saturday: 11-11; Sunday: 12-10.30*
Food: *Monday-Friday: 12-2.15 and 5-7.30*
🌼 ☎ ℗
☎ *020 8472 2351*
Plaistow tube and buses 69, 241, 262, 325 and 473
Beers: *regulars are Courage Best and Directors. Guest beers vary and might include selections from the Adnams range, Fuller's London Pride, Everards and Smiles.*

Plaistow is probably the last place you'd expect to stumble across a 16th century coaching inn, once frequented by the most famous highwayman of all, Dick Turpin – but then life can be full of surprises.

Although the frontage was rebuilt in 1875, many parts of this two bar pub are original. Catering for all tastes, there's a jukebox in one room while the second is a music free zone. Attached to the pub is the famous West Ham Boxing Club, which has spawned such notable boxers as Terry Spinks, the first Briton to win an Olympic boxing gold. There's also a large garden and a function room available for hire.

The wide range of beers incorporates a varied list of guests and food includes fresh cod or plaice, home made steak and kidney pie or pudding and various daily specials, while vegetarians might choose savoury cheese flan served with vegetables of the day.

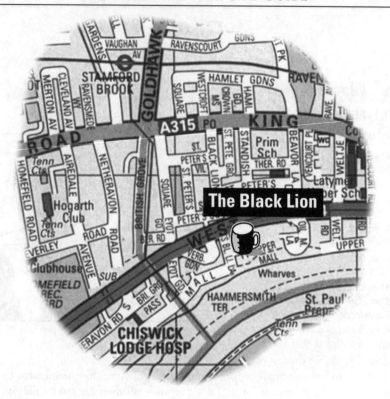

The Black Lion

E14

The Ferry House

26 Ferry Street, Isle of Dogs

Open: Monday-Saturday: 11-11; Sunday: 12-10.30
Food: Monday-Saturday: 11-6; Sunday: no meals but there is free seafood all day
☻
☎ 020 7537 9587
Island Gardens Docklands Light Railway
Beers: Courage Best

The oldest pub on the Isle of Dogs, the small and cosy Ferry House dates back to 1822. Family-run by a couple who only took over last winter, already they seem to have embraced one of the better East End pub traditions of offering free morsels of food on Sundays – in this case it's seafood, available all day long on the bar. Otherwise, sustenance is a simple affair of crusty bread sandwiches or freshly cooked jacket potatoes.

The Grapes

76 Narrow Street, Limehouse

Open: Monday-Friday: 12-3, 5.30-11; Saturday: 7-11; Sunday: 12-3, 7-10.30
Food: Monday-Friday: 12-2 and 7-9; Saturday: 7-9; Sunday: 12-3. There is also a separate fish restaurant
☘
☎ *020 7987 4396*
Limehouse or West Ferry Docklands Light Railway
Beers: Regulars are Adnams, Burton Ale and Marston's Pedigree. Guests include Greene King IPA and Abbot Ale.

Standing on the River Thames, Dickensian is the word most often used about the Grapes, perhaps not surprisingly as the writer used it as the model for his pub, The Six Jolly Fellowship Porters in *Our Mutual Friend*. In the novel, drunken customers were rowed out to the middle of the river, drowned and their corpses sold to anatomists for dissection. I think that's what's called going overboard on the ale.

There's been a tavern on site since the 16th century, but much of the area was destroyed by fire and the present pub dates from around 1720. Featuring large windows overlooking the river, there's also an outside veranda that stands on stilts in the water. As such, the pub offers a wonderful vantage point, exploited to the full by painter Rex Whistler, who visited regularly to capture the view on canvas.

Back inside, there's a long, narrow and wooden interior, which boasts no jukebox, gaming machines, pool, darts or any other distractions from the good range of cask conditioned beers. In theory, you may find yourself jostling for space at the bar with some of the pub's more famous neighbours, including politician David Owen and actors Ian McKellan and Steven Berkoff.

Food includes fish and proper chips, fish cakes and new potatoes and bangers and mash. There are also vegetarian soups or a ploughman's. Upstairs there's a well-known and celebrated fish restaurant, where it's advisable to book in advance.

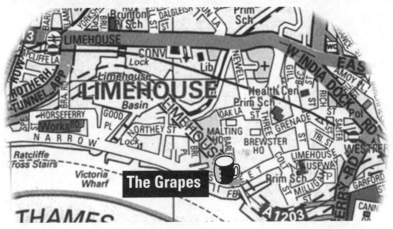

The Pier Tavern

299 Manchester Road, Isle of Dogs

Open: *Monday-Saturday: 12-11;*
Sunday: 12-10.30
Food: *Monday-Friday: 12-3 and*
5.30-9.30; Saturday: 12-7;
Sunday: 12-9.30
ﬆ ❀ ♿

☎ *020 7515 9528*

Island Gardens Docklands Light
Railway and buses D8 and D6
Beers: *Morland's Old Speckled*
Hen, Fuller's London Pride,
Wadworth 6X and Marston's
Pedigree are available regularly
plus one guest.

The Pier is most famous for its
resident ghost, Ginger, who is
reputedly a dockworker, accidentally killed at Millwall Docks.

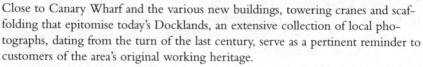

Close to Canary Wharf and the various new buildings, towering cranes and scaf-
folding that epitomise today's Docklands, an extensive collection of local photographs, dating from the turn of the last century, serve as a pertinent reminder to
customers of the area's original working heritage.

The pub was first registered as an alehouse in 1842 and features a traditional looking exterior with award-winning floral displays in the summer. The interior is a
well kept, traditionally furnished food tavern with a separate restaurant area.
There's a roomy main bar, with wooden floors and fittings, and a first floor bar
available for private hire. The pub hosts regular quiz nights and live music every
Saturday.

Food includes swordfish steak, Cumberland sausages and chicken Caesar salad,
while vegetarians can choose from tasty options like Thai red vegetable curry or
Mediterranean risotto.

E17

The Flower Pot

128 Wood Street, Walthamstow

Open: *Monday-Saturday: 12-11; Sunday: 12-10.30*
Food: *None*
 ♿ ✽ ♞
☏ *020 8223 9941*
Wood Street railway station and buses W16 and W15
Beers: *Bass is available as a regular while guests might include Young's.*

If you like a reliably good pint of Bass in an old-fashioned pub that doesn't even bother with food, then the Flower Pot is for you.

A longstanding *Good Beer Guide* entrant, many of the customers have been coming to this small but comfortable Victorian pub for more than 20 years. Entertainment includes bar billiards and live music once a fortnight.

BARKING

The Britannia

1 Church Road

Open: *Monday-Friday: 11-3 and 5-11; Saturday: 12-11; Sunday: 12-10.30*
Food: *Monday to Friday: 12-2; Monday to Thursday: 5-8; no food on Friday evening or Sat; Sun 12-2.45*
✽ Ⓟ
☏ *020 8594 1305*
Barking railway
Beers: *Young's Bitter, Special, Triple A. Guests include Young's Winter Warmer.*

In an area that could be viewed as a bit of a real ale desert, this is a deservedly popular locals pub, winning the local CAMRA pub of the year award in 2000, in addition to awards in 1995 and 1996. There's a spacious saloon, a basic public bar and live music some weekends. On the menu might be liver and bacon, beef curry, chicken tikka masala, vegetable pie and various sandwiches.

HORNCHURCH

Chequers

North Street

Open: Monday-Saturday: 11-11; Sunday: 12-10.30
Food: Monday to Friday – check with pub for times. None on Sat or Sunday
& ℗
☎ 01708 442094
Emerson Park railway and buses 256, 370 and 373
Beers: Ansells Best, Greene King Abbot Ale, Friary Meux and Young's.

A small, old-fashioned Victorian local, the Chequers is renowned for its well-kept beer and busy but friendly atmosphere. Indeed, the South West Essex branch of CAMRA gave it their ultimate accolade, choosing it as their pub of the year three years running, in 1997, 1998 and 1999. Food is standard pub nosh of burgers – with a vegetarian option – pizzas and ploughmans. Look out for the occasional famous footballer.

WOODFORD GREEN

Cricketers

299-301 High Road

Open: Monday-Saturday: 11-11; Sunday: 12-10.30
Food: Monday-Friday: 12-2; Saturday: 12-2
❀ ℗
☎ 020 8504 2734
South Woodford railway
Beers: McMullen AK, Country, Gladstone and seasonal beers.

Standing close to the famous statue of Sir Winston Churchill on the green, this comfortable, friendly, suburban local offers a range of home made food specials and is well known for the quality of its pies. A two bar pub, there's a wood panelled lounge and a public bar. A previous CAMRA pub of the year, fans of pub quizzes should note that there's one held here on the last Tuesday of every month.

Travellers Friend

496 High Road

Open: Monday-Friday: 11-11; Saturday: 12-11; Sunday: 12-4, 7-10.30
Food: Monday-Friday: 12-2; Saturday: 12-2

 ♿ ✿ Ⓟ

☎ *020 8504 2435*

Woodford tube station and buses 20, 179 and W13

Beers: Ridleys IPA, Courage Best and Directors, Greene King Abbot Ale, Fuller's London Pride and Adnams Broadside are regularly available. Guest beers may come from Ridley, Adnams or Brains.

Featured in CAMRA's *Good Beer Guide* for the last 11 years, the couple who run this small, very friendly local, described as "a little gem", proudly boast that they have never sold keg beer.

The interior features wood panelling and snob screens and pub games provide the entertainment, rather than gaming machines, music or television. Near to Epping Forest, dogs are welcome as long as they are on a lead.

Food includes home made pies and warming curries in winter and there are omelettes and pasta dishes for vegetarians.

ILFORD

...also worth trying

Prince of Wales

63 Green Lane (Ilford railway)
Although it's 15 minutes walk from the local railway station, this is a thriving locals pub, with two separate bars, serving Adnams Bitter, Tetley, Burton Ale and usually two or three changing guest beers.

North London

N1

The Albion

10 Thornhill Road, Barnsbury

Open: Monday-Saturday: 12-11; Sunday: 12-10.30
Food: Monday-Friday: 12-3 and 6-9.30; Sat and Sunday: 12-9.30
& ❀ Ch: weekends only until 6pm if eating with parents
☎ 020 7607 7450
Angel tube
Beers: Theakston Best Bitter

Lesser mortals rub shoulders with wannabes and soap stars in this deservedly popular Islington local. Yet while you may find yourself saying Hi de Hi to actress Su Pollard – who is a regular customer – most of the clientele are here to enjoy the cosy traditional ambience rather than autograph hunt.

The inside of this deceptively large pub has a country feel, with horse brasses, hunting prints and copper pans, but the pub really comes into its own in the summer months, when you can sit outside in the large garden and bask in the rare British sunshine.

Food options are pub standards but served in large portions and might include steak and ale pie, fish and chips and sausage and mash, while vegetarians could choose dishes like broccoli and three cheese pasta melt and tortellini with roasted red pepper sauce.

Camden Head

2 Camden Walk

Open: Monday-Saturday: 11-11; Sunday: 12-10.30
Food: Monday-Sunday: 12-9
& ❀
☎ 020 7359 0851
Angel tube
Beers: Courage Best, Directors and guest ales, including Charles Wells Bombardier and Shepherd Neame's Spitfire.

At the heart of Islington's antiques market, the Camden Head dates back to 1806 and retains many of its original features, including fireplaces, Corinthian columns and engraved windows.

This lively pub attracts a mixed clientele of stallholders, those seeking respite from bargain hunting and, during weekdays, office workers. Entertainment includes comedy evenings held on Monday, Thursday, Friday and Saturday and a quiz every Tuesday. Watch out for the resident ghost called George.

Food includes beef and ale pie, Cajun chicken and a Sunday roast. Options for non-meat eaters are roasted red pepper lasagne, sandwiches, nachos and fries with different toppings.

Compton Arms

4 Compton Avenue

Open: Monday-Saturday: 12-11; Sunday: 12-10.30
Food: Monday-Sunday: 12-2.30 and 6-9, except there is no food on Tuesday evenings
 ♿ ❊ ♰
✆ 020 7359 6883
Highbury and Islington tube
Beers: Greene King IPA, Abbot Ale and Triumph.

This small cottage style pub, with its low, beamed ceiling, dimpled windows and woodwork, is a little taste of the countryside in the otherwise fashionable urban landscape that is Islington. Popular with regulars, to the extent that it can get quite crowded, particularly at weekends, the television is only switched on when there's an important football match to watch – but don't worry, this is no raucous sports bar.

Regular food options include sausage and mash, but with six different kinds of specially made sausages available – including Toulouse, Pork and Stilton and Cumberland – there's almost one for every day of the week. There are also lots of veggie choices, including mushroom and nut fettuccini, three cheese pasta bake and vegetable chilli.

The Crown

116 Cloudesley Road

Open: Monday-Saturday: 12-11; Sunday: 12-10.30
Food: Monday-Saturday: 12-3 and 6.30-10; Sunday: 12-3.30
 ♿ ❊ ♰
✆ 020 8996 2000
Angel tube
Beers: All are from the Fuller's range and include London Pride, Summer Ale, Jack Frost, Red Fox and Honeydew.

Originally built in 1828, the Crown had become a slightly jaded local, but has recently undergone a metamorphosis into what the manager calls "a Bohemian gastro pub". Sofas, wooden chairs and tables and modern lighting have joined its listed features, engraved glass and wood panelling, to create a modern hybrid featuring a funk jazz soundtrack.

There is the usual range of Fuller's ales on tap, including seasonal variations, and the food is decidedly upmarket, reflecting its newly acquired aspirations. The menu changes every six weeks but might include pan-fried chicken breast in polenta crumb with sweet pepper sauce, char grilled rump steak with root vegetables, chips and a red wine and mushroom sauce, gnocchi with saffron and aubergine puree and red onion, black olive and ricotta cheese tart.

The Dove Regent

65 Graham Street

Open: Monday to Thursday: 12-11; Friday and Saturday: 12-10.30 and Sunday: 12-10.30
Food: Monday to Thursday: 12-11; Friday and Saturday: 12-12 and Sunday: 12-10.30
♿ ☎, *but no nappy changing facilities*
☎ *020 7275 7617*
Old Street or Angel tube
Beers: Boddingtons plus a wide range of Belgian beers on draft, including Hoegaarden, Leffe Blond and Leffe Brun, Bellevue Kriek and Bellevue Gueuze and De Koninck, plus a different guest beer each month. Bottled beers include trappist and abbey ales, fruit beers and regional varieties.

Open since 1999, this is the newest addition to the Dove group of free houses and, like its sister pub in Hackney, it too offers an environment free from sexism, racism and homophobia. And as if to prove the point that a good laugh shouldn't be at someone else's expense, the pub plays host to regular comedy evenings.

On Thursday, there is the recommended "On the Tiles" while the longstanding Meccano Comedy Club has its home here on Friday and Saturday nights. Other entertainment in the Dove Regent – decorated in the livery colours of George IV during the Regency period – includes a quiz night on Wednesdays where two Eurostar tickets to Belgium and a trip around a brewery is the star prize. To further the European feel, there's a French table football game and the pub plans to hold regular music nights in the future.

Food is given high priority and the daily changing menu might include corn chowder, lamb shoulder for two, red snapper with a red onion and cranberry glaze and butternut pumpkin with a lime and pesto dressing. On Sundays there's a traditional roast lunch with meat free or fish alternatives. Other options make the most of the pub's Belgian beers, for example there are specially made sausages incorporating beer and mussels cooked in different beers.

The Duke of Cambridge

30 St Peter's Street

Open: M: 5-11; Tuesday to Saturday: 12-11 and Sunday: 12-10.30
Food: M: 7-10.30; Tuesday to Saturday: 12.30-3 and 6.30-10.30; Sunday: 12.30-3.30 and 6.30-10
❀ ☂
☎ *020 7359 1877*
Angel tube and buses to Essex Road and Upper Street
Beers: All are organic and regulars include Pitfield's Singhboulton, Eco Warrior and Black Eagle and St Peter's Organic Ale. There's a wide range of bottled beers, including Sam Smith's, Bucher and Sade.

The Duke of Cambridge has the unusual distinction of being the first certified organic pub in the UK.

It's the brainchild of the pioneering partnership of Geetie Singh and Esther Boulton, who believed they could run an organic gastro pub which reflected their environmental and ethical principles, but still make money – and thankfully, they were right.

Set in a side street, just a few minutes walk from Islington's trendy Upper Street, and originally built in 1851, the Duke of Cambridge has stripped floors, plain walls and second hand mismatched tables and chairs. To that end, they've forged links with a local company who tip them the wink if they spot anything good.

Large windows overlook the street and the pub has been carefully restored retaining as many original features as possible, including the name. Indeed, the duo feels particularly strongly that pub names should never be changed as they are an integral part of the local heritage. That's a view that I wish more pub owners shared, particularly those who insist on rechristening their new acquisition The Sozzled Rat and Iguana. To continue the old style traditional feel, there are no fruit machines, games or music.

All the beers on offer are organic, with the local Pitfield brewery supplying three choices, including the pub's own Singhboulton. As their award-winning status demonstrates – they were winners of the Time Out Gastro Pub 2000 – there's a clear emphasis on food, reflected in the fact that when I visited, virtually every customer was eating. The menu changes twice daily, features entirely organic produce and might include chicken liver paté, served with pickles, relish and toast, a soup, chicken in red wine with bacon, onions and mash or baked smoked haddock with leek mash and cheese sauce. There are always two vegetarian dishes and a range of yummy deserts, like pear and almond tart with cream or chocolate soufflé cake with crème fraiche.

In essence, the Duke of Cambridge takes the best of the past and gives it a contemporary twist to create a pub that is both traditional and forward-looking. It's no mean feat but, judging by the droves of customers they are attracting and the opening of a sister pub in the East End, they've pulled it off.

The Eagle

2 Shepherdess Walk, Hoxton

Open: Monday-Friday: 12-11; closed Saturday and Sunday
Food: Monday-Friday: 12-9
&. ❀
☎ *020 7553 7681*
Old Street tube
Beers: Bass and Fuller's London Pride are regularly available while seasonal ales might include Greene King IPA and Marston's Pedigree.

This fine traditional Victorian pub is immortalised in the famous nursery rhyme, in the verse that says: "Up and down the City Road, in and out the Eagle, that's the way the money goes, Pop goes the Weasel".

Built on the site of the celebrated Victorian Grecian theatre and pleasure gardens, which is remembered with a blue plaque on the outside wall, around half of the original building remains. Renowned performers include the music hall legend, Marie Lloyd, who made her first public appearance here in 1885.

Food is a cut above the usual pub fare and might include salmon and garlic king prawns, spicy chicken breast with pan-fried peppers and stuffed mozzarella field mushrooms.

Hemingford Arms

Hemingford Road

Open: Monday-Saturday: 11-11; Sunday: 12-10.30
Food: Monday-Friday: 12-3; 6.30-10; Saturday: 6.30-10.30; Sunday: 6.30-10
☎ *020 7607 3303*
Caledonian Road railway station and bus 153
Beers: Regulars are Courage Directors and Best, Morland's Old Speckled Hen and Wadworth's 6X. Guest beers include Boddingtons.

If you're searching for The Rocky Road to Dublin or you've been a Wild Rover, the Hemingford Arms could be just the place for a pit stop. The pub plays host to a varied musical menu of traditional Irish and Scottish folk, blue grass or even hits from the 60s every evening except Thursday, when there's a quiz.

Presumably the landlord ran out of storage space for all those old knick knacks he's collected over the years, as ice skates, French horns, stuffed animals and even a baby's pram hang from the ceiling. At lunchtimes traditional pub grub, like cottage pie, is on offer but in the evening it's replaced by Thai food, including various vegetarian alternatives.

The Hope and Anchor

207 Upper Street

Open: *Monday-Saturday: 12-1am
and Sunday: 12-12*
Food: *Monday-Friday: 12-3; 5-7*
☎ *020 7354 1312*
*Highbury and Islington tube and
buses 4, 19, 43*
Beers: *Greene King IPA and
Abbot Ale.*

Ask anyone who looks like
they might be old enough to
have a Sex Pistol's album lurk-
ing in their record collection
whether they remember the
Hope and Anchor, and it's
guaranteed they'll turn misty-
eyed.

One of the most famous live music venues in the capital, past acts who have
played here include Madness, the Stranglers, Ash and yes, you guessed it, those
infamous anarchists in the UK. For those of us who are close to swapping our
punk leather jacket for a comfortable all weather anorak, it's probably best to stick
to the ground floor, where the walls are covered in all kinds of music memorabilia
featuring the many who found fame and fortune after strutting their stuff here.

Meanwhile, those who make it downstairs to the brick clad basement, will discover that the musical tradition continues unabated, as the pub plays host to three
live bands every night. So if all you're seeking is a quiet pint of one of Greene
King's two best-selling ales and a trip down memory lane, it's probably best to
visit during the hours of daylight.

Food is standard pub grub and includes sausage and mash, cod and chips, steak
and kidney pie, veggie burgers and jacket potatoes.

Kings Head Theatre Pub

115 Upper Street

Open: *Monday to Thursday: 11-1; Friday and Saturday: 12-2 and Sunday: 12-1*
Food: *Tue-Saturday: 12-3; Sunday: 12-7*
♿
☎ *020 7226 0364*
Angel and Highbury and Islington tube; buses 4, 19, 30 and 43
Beers: *Adnams, Burton, Young's and Benskins all available regularly.*

Fear not, you haven't gone bonkers or inadvertently stepped back in time, for the Kings Head really does still use pounds, shillings and pence, rather than that new fangled decimal currency.

There's no jukebox, pool table or gambling machines but there is live music every night of the year, except Christmas Day, based around the piano in the front bar of this incredibly lively Victorian pub. They've used the same formula for years, but clearly it's a winning one, judging by the droves of Islington trendies, students and "resting" luvvies who hang out at London's oldest theatre bar every evening.

The food is a cut above the usual pub fodder and includes interesting options like Kerala fish curry, seafood soup, chilli chicken and a vegetarian thali that includes dal and rice. It's an Islington institution – but I'd hate to be a member of the bar staff.

Marquess Tavern

32 Canonbury Street

Open: Monday-Saturday: 11-11 and Sunday: 12-10.30
Food: Monday-Saturday: 12-9.30
❀
☎ *020 7354 2975*
Highbury and Islington tube and Essex Road railway
Beers: All from the Young's range, including Bitter, Special, Triple A and Winter Warmer. Bottle conditioned beers include Special London Ale.

In theory I could walk from my house in Hertfordshire to the Marquess Tavern in Islington as both back on to the New River, built more than 400 years ago to bring water from the county's springs to the City of London.

Back in the 1980s, when *Good Beer Guide* editor Roger Protz compiled the original CAMRA guide to London's best pubs, I accompanied him on his visit to the Marquess. "What do you think of the décor?" he asked me. "It's like a Turkish brothel" I replied, in my best Birmingham twang – and of course he couldn't resist immortalising my view in print. With the benefit of hindsight, I'd like to think that perhaps now I might say that the brass lamps, mirrors and high curved ceiling foster a feeling of opulence, grandeur and elegance. But I expect the truth lies somewhere in between.

Voted CAMRA's north London pub of the year in 1998, the Marquess has a well-deserved reputation amongst its regulars for providing a reliably good pint of Young's beers in comfortable 19th century surroundings. Entertainment includes a hotly-contested, well-established quiz, held on the first Monday of every month. Food includes a daily roast with all the trimmings, filled mushrooms with salad and fries and sausages, served with bubble and squeak and onion gravy.

Wenlock Arms

26 Wenlock Road

Open: *Monday-Saturday: 11-11 and Sunday: 12-10.30*
Food: *Monday-Saturday: 12-10; Sunday: 12-8*

🏇

☎ *020 7608 3406*

Old Street tube and buses 43 and 214

Beers: *a huge range of up to eight real ales plus one real cider or perry. Adnams is always on offer and guests might include Crouch Vale, Nethergate, Pitfield, O'Hanlons, Holt's and Hydes. There is always at least one mild. Bottled beers include Erdinger, Chimay, Duvel and Worthington White Shield.*

Real ale lovers who are lucky enough to find themselves in the Wenlock Arms may think they've died and gone to heaven. Built in 1835, this corner local tucked away just off City Road, has as many of its original features preserved as possible, including its coal fire.

But at the pub's heart lies its love of beer. There are up to eight real ales on tap at any one time, lovingly tended by the CAMRA stalwarts who run the pub, and the choice often features local micro breweries, like Pitfield and O'Hanlon. And as if that wasn't enough, there is always at least one real cider or perry and a mild – a bit of a rarity in the bitter dominated south of England. Not surprisingly, the Wenlock Arms is a regular in CAMRA's *Good Beer Guide*.

Added attractions include a pub quiz on Thursday and live jazz or blues sessions on Friday and Saturday. On Sundays, there's jazz piano. Food features the pub's famous salt beef "sandwedges", hot sausage sarnies and real Cornish or vegetarian pasties.

N2

The Windsor Castle

The Walks, Finchley

Open: *Monday-Friday: 11-11; Saturday: 11-11; Sunday: 12-10.30*
Food: *Monday-Saturday: 12-2 and 7-9; Sunday: 7-9*

♿ ❀ 🏇 ℗

☎ *020 8883 5763*

East Finchley tube

Beers: *McMullen's Country Bitter, AK, Gladstone, Courage Directors and Bass.*

Just off Finchley High Street, the Windsor Castle is a friendly one room local with a patio area. There is live music on Saturday night and a quiz evening held every Thursday. The home cooked food includes home roast ham, jacket potatoes, mixed grills, omelettes, vegetarian burgers and salads.

N6

...also worth trying

Flask Tavern

77 Highgate West Hill, Highgate (Highgate/Archway tube)
Very famous and popular 17th century pub with a warren of small rooms on different levels and flagstone floors, used by a variety of famous – and infamous – people down the centuries, including highwayman Dick Turpin, William Hogarth and Karl Marx. There's a wide selection of beers including Adnams, Greene King Abbot Ale, Morland's Old Speckled Hen and others.

N8

The Queens

26 Broadway Parade, Crouch End

Open: Monday-Friday: 11-11; Saturday: 11-11; Sunday: 12-10.30
Food: Monday-Saturday: 11 'til late; Sunday: 12-6
❀
☎ 020 8340 2031
Finsbury Park tube and rail, Turnpike Lane tube and buses 41 and 91
Beers: Courage Best and Directors.

I discovered the Queens one Friday evening, when the search for a decent pub was proving to be akin to finding the Holy Grail. We'd found theme pubs, yoof pubs and pubs where nothing was drinkable, but nowhere seemed to offer an old-fashioned good night out, where even those of us who are a bit past our sell by date can let our hair down and have some fun at the end of a long hard week. And then we stumbled upon the Queens...

A century old, but still good-looking, it's a great melting pot of a pub, where chilled-out musicians hang out with raucous brickies and badge-wearing eco-warriors sit side by side with married, mortgaged but still 'mad for it' 40-some-things. Everyone shares the simple wish to have as good a time as possible. On Friday and Sunday nights the joint is jumping with live free bands playing music ranging from jazz and folk to stadium style rock – you name it and almost any-thing goes. Meanwhile Thursday and Saturday nights offer wannabe pop stars the chance to entertain, with well-established and very popular karaoke.

The pub itself is listed inside and out and has three separate areas, one with a small stage at the end, where the bands perform. The décor features stained glass windows, ornate ceilings, lots of dark wood and red carpets and padded seats. Food is simple pub grub and includes an all day breakfast, burgers or fish with chips, jacket potatoes and filled baps. But frankly, if you go there to eat and admire the architecture, you're missing the point. Note that, at the time of going to press, part of the pub was under the threat of being turned into a pizza parlour. Let's hope that, by the time you read this, sanity will have prevailed.

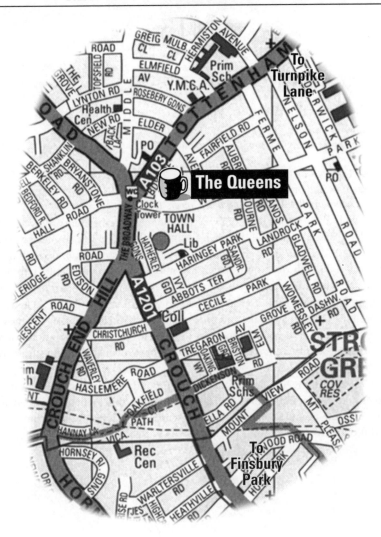

N13

The Woodman

128 Bourne Hill, Palmers Green

Open: Monday-Saturday: 11-11; Sunday: 12-10.30
Food: Monday-Saturday: 11-3 and 6-9; Sunday: 12-3
❀ ☎ Ⓟ
☎ 020 8882 0294
Southgate tube and bus W9
Beers: Caledonian 80%, Worthington and Flowers IPA.

Originally built as a cottage in 1727, retired police sergeant Henry Wale was first granted a license to sell ale in his front room in 1868. The rest, as they say, is history, as the Woodman has been a pub ever since. A friendly local, decorated in a traditional style with open fires, there's live music once a month and a pub quiz held in the winter months.

There's a full menu of food, including pan-fried lamb cutlets, fresh poached salmon, blue cheese pasta bake and broccoli and potato cheese bake. For those whose taste buds have yet to encompass the sun dried tomato revolution, there's also a special 'step back in time' fixed menu of prawn cocktail, sirloin steak and black forest gateau.

Nearby is a small green where an old wooden pound still stands. This was used to keep any stray pigs, horses or cows from getting into mischief and provided an income for the pound keeper (or pinder), who would demand a fee from the rightful owner for the animal's release.

N16

The Daniel Defoe

102 Stoke Newington Church Street

Open: Monday-Saturday: 12-11; Sunday: 12-10.30
Food: Monday-Friday: 5-8; Saturday: 12-3; Sunday: 12-4
♿ ❂
☏ *020 7254 2906*
Stoke Newington railway, bus 73
Beers: *Charles Wells Eagle, Bombardier and Defoe Ale are available regularly. Guests might include Marston's Pedigree and Morland's Old Speckled Hen.*

Once known as Steptoes and before that the Clarence, the pub was refurbished in the autumn of 2000 and with it came another name change to the Daniel Defoe. At least there's a local connection in that the author of Robinson Crusoe was born in Stokey. The eponymously named pub is a well-maintained and pleasant local, serving Charles Wells beers. There's live music fortnightly and karaoke every month.

The home cooked food includes steak and ale pie and Sunday roast. There's also bangers and mash, featuring more unusual sausages than most, such as chicken and apricot and beef and Guinness. There's a choice of at least four daily vegetarian specials that might include Mediterranean pasta bake, mushroom and red pepper stroganoff and vegetable jambalaya.

The Rose and Crown

199 Stoke Newington Church Street

Open: *Monday-Saturday: 11.30-11; Sunday: 12-10.30*
Food: *Monday-Friday: 12-2.30; Sunday: 12-4*
ら ☎
☎ *020 7254 7497*
Manor House tube, Stoke Newington railway and bus 73
Beers: *Adnams, Marston's Pedigree and Ruddles County are available regularly.*
Although you're firmly in the middle of Norf Landon, you could almost be convinced that the Rose and Crown is a pleasant backwater pub – providing you don't look out of the listed opaque glass windows and can shut your ears to the occasional police sirens.

With its two open fires in winter – one of them almost perpetually hogged by the pub's dog – and many original features including wood panelling and a listed ceiling and doors, this street corner local proudly brags that its well-tended real ales are its best sellers. Once four rooms, it's been opened into one for as long as I can remember, but somehow it manages to retain the feel of having several different drinking areas.

Although there's no music in the evenings, there are regular music quizzes that have elicited a great following and a monthly pub quiz, which also attracts the hordes. The pub is also famous for its Sunday roasts – lamb, beef, pork, chicken and turkey – while other homemade food includes steak pie, beef bourguignon and two daily vegetarian specialities, including vegetarian sausage and mash, carrot and coriander goujons and pasta bake. There's also a guest house, regularly used by the London office of Greenpeace to accommodate their visitors. Now how right on is that?

N21

The Dog and Duck

74 Hopper's Road, Winchmore Hill

Open: Monday-Saturday: 11-11; Sunday: 12-10.30
Food: None
❀ ⛾ *in the beer garden*
☎ 020 8886 1987
Southgate tube, Winchmore Hill/Palmers Green railway and bus W9
Beers: Greene King IPA, Young's Special, Wadworth 6X and Boddingtons are available regularly. These may be supplemented by various seasonal ales.

Known locally as the 'woof and quack', this is a single bar back street pub in a terraced cottage dating from the turn-of-the-century. Although it's had a recent refurbishment, it's lost none of its character and the largely 30-something locals have remained loyal. Entertainment includes Saturday night music, fortnightly jazz and a fortnightly quiz. There's a secluded beer garden and a shove ha'penny board. The pub is a previous winner of the local CAMRA branch Pub of the Year award.

The Orange Tree

18 Highfield Road, Winchmore Hill

Open: Monday-Saturday: 11-11; Sunday: 12-10.30
Food: Monday-Friday: 12-2.30; Saturday: All day; Sunday: 12-2.30
♿ ❀ ⛾ *in the beer garden*
☎ 020 8360 4853
Winchmore Hill railway and bus 329
Beers: Greene King IPA, Ruddles County and Best are available regularly. Guests include Bateman's and Fuller's Chiswick.

The winner of the local CAMRA Pub of the Year Award in both 1999 and 2000, this petite and pretty local pub in a residential area, just off Green Lanes, is what the landlord describes as a 'dying breed', hardly altering over the last 50 years. Continuity is no mean feat in the face of the constantly changing themes, fads and fancies that characterise much of today's licensed trade.

The large garden has a play area and barbeque and there's occasional live music, a disco and pub quiz. Food is reasonably priced and includes sausage and mash, vegetable lasagne, burgers, and cheese and broccoli bake.

N22

The Phoenix Bar

Alexandra Palace and Park, Wood Green

Open: *Monday-Sunday: 10.30 –11, but alcohol is only sold during the permitted hours*
Food: *Monday-Friday: 10.30-6; Sat and Sunday: 10.30-8*
& ❀ ✇ Ⓟ
☎ *020 8365 2121*
Wood Green tube, Alexandra Palace railway and bus W3
Beers: *Fuller's ESB, Adnams Bitter and Broadside, Tetley Bitter, Marston's Pedigree and Crouch Vale are all available regularly. Guests might include Fuller's Summer Ale and Red Fox or Crouch Vale's Conqueror.*

Set in the 196–acre grounds of Ally Pally, the Phoenix glories in breathtaking panoramic views of London's skyline. On a clear day, you can see forever – or at least as far away as Canary Wharf and Crystal Palace.

The People's Palace first opened in 1873, providing entertainment and recreation to the Victorians but sadly, 16 days later, it burnt down. A rebuilt version opened less than two years later and in 1935 the BBC saw its potential and leased part of it, making the world's first public television transmissions from here a year later. It remained the Beeb's main broadcasting centre until 1956, after which it was used exclusively for news.

There was a second fire in 1980 but eventually the Palace re-opened in 1988. Today, Ally Pally is the venue for regular exhibitions and fairs, conferences and banquets. The park has a pitch and putt golf course, boating lake, children's playground, animal enclosure and fun fairs during the summer. And despite the Palace's propensity to burst into flames, it continues to play with fire, hosting a spectacular annual fireworks display that draws the crowds from miles around – bear in mind that parking is a nightmare.

The aptly named pub is part of the complex, opening onto the Palm Court foyer, with its tinkling fountains and foliage. Every year it joins in Ally Pally's beer and food festival, held as part of the Bonfire Night celebrations. Open for full English breakfast every day, other reasonably priced food options include scampi and chips, filled baguettes, baked potatoes and lasagne. Look out for occasional live jazz evenings with Big Al's Jazzers.

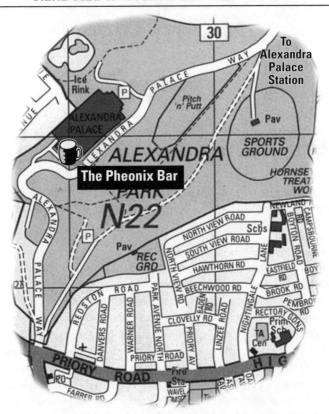

The Starting Gate

Station Road, Wood Green

Open: Monday-Saturday: 12-11; Sunday: 12-10
Food: Monday-Saturday: 12-3 and 6-9; Sunday: 12-9
※ ⛄
☎ *020 8889 9789*
Wood Green tube and Alexandra Palace railway
Beers: *Tetley Bitter, Marston's Pedigree and Young's Special are all available regularly. Guest beers include Burton Ale, Fuller's London Pride, Ansells and Morland's Old Speckled Hen.*

Step out of Alexandra Palace railway station, cross the road and you're under starters orders for a reliably well-kept pint in this listed 125 year-old local. There's an island bar, especially fine wood and glass workmanship, a few pot plants and lots of friendly regulars. A popular weekly rollover quiz is held every Tuesday and the licensee is hopeful that his plans to open an upstairs theatre later this year will get the go-ahead. Food includes Sunday roast, mushroom pizza and a curry menu.

North West

NW1

The Engineer

65 Gloucester Avenue

Open: Monday-Saturday: 9-11 and Sunday: 9-10.30
Food: Monday-Sunday: 9-11
 ♿ ⚘ ☎
☎ *020 7722 0950*
Chalk Farm and Camden Town tube and bus 274
Beers: Morland's Old Speckled Hen and Fuller's London Pride are available regularly.

The Engineer is one of London's burgeoning band of gastro pubs, where the focus is clearly on imaginative food, served in slightly more laid-back surroundings than a restaurant, but with the same emphasis on quality and style.

An 18th century building, this Primrose Hill pub was formerly the home of the ultimate English engineer, Isambard Kingdom Brunel, designer of the Clifton Suspension Bridge, various railway lines, bridges and tunnels and three steamships.

On the menu might be Moroccan fishcakes, wild rice kedgeree, sirloin steak or beetroot and potato rosti with wild mushrooms and apple compote. It's probably worth booking, particularly if it's a nice day and you'd like to eat in the garden.

The Head of Steam

1 Eversholt Street

Open: Monday-Saturday: 11-11 and Sunday: 12-10.30
Food: Monday-Friday: 12-2.30 and 5-8; Saturday: 12-3 and Sunday: 12-4
☎, until 9pm
☎ *020 7383 3359*
Euston tube and Euston railway. Buses 10, 73, 91, 59, 68, 168, 253 and 30
Beers: Shepherd Neame Masterbrew, Hopback Summer Lightning, Holt's Bitter, O'Hanlons, Brakspear and Cottage are all available regularly. Guests might include Caledonian Deuchars IPA and 80 shillings, Eccleshall Slaters Top Totty and Black Sheep Special and Bitter. There are regular themed beer festivals. Gale's Prize Old Ale is also available.

I suspect that would-be rail travelers, thwarted in their journey by non existent or eternally delayed trains, think of this little pub, which is just outside Euston station's main concourse, as a life-saver.

But it's much more than just a relatively pleasant place to watch the clock tick, as it offers a lovingly cared for, eclectic and constantly changing choice of real ales, all served by friendly and knowledgeable bar staff. The range often features small micros and usually includes that rare breed in the south of England: a dark mild. There's also traditional Biddenden cider on draught. Its efforts on behalf of fans of the real stuff have not gone unnoticed by CAMRA, who declared it North London Pub of the Year in 1999.

The first floor bar has wooden floorboards and lots of wooden chairs and tables and there's a raised no smoking area at the back. The walls are decorated with old railway memorabilia, including station signs, lamps, uniforms, signals and prints that depict trains on the move, presumably to show those who have abandoned all hope that it is possible. For those who think that buying their own train might provide a cheaper and more reliable alternative, you can invest in a model one here, as well as mugs, t-shirts and other souvenirs of that bygone age when British rail travel was par excellence. Buy it and weep.

Food includes bangers and mash, fish and chips, steak baguette and veggie chilli and rice.

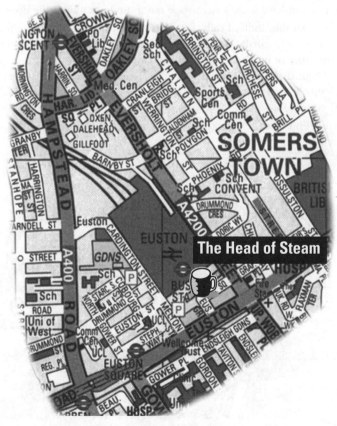

The Spread Eagle

141 Albert Street, Camden Town

Open: Monday-Saturday: 11-11 and Sunday: 12-10.30
Food: Monday-Saturday: 12-7.30; Sunday: 12-5
❀

☎ *020 7267 1410*

Camden Town tube and buses 274 and C2

Beers: Young's Bitter, Special and Triple A are all regularly available. Seasonal beers include Winter Warmer.

Fads may come and go, but the Spread Eagle remains a constant in the otherwise changing landscape of style-conscious Camden Town.

I've been drinking here for almost 20 years and have yet to have a bad pint or a less than pleasant evening – although I must confess to having missed more films than I care to remember at the nearby cinemas, as the lure of the pub has proved too much for me to leave the comfort of my seat to queue for a ticket. However, chancing upon the pub's occasional football quiz, run from October through to December, might have helped encourage me to find my way to the door.

Apparently what the landlord calls 'Brit pop types' have discovered the pub's charms and are occasionally in evidence, but generally it attracts a less affected crowd than many of its Camden Town contemporaries. Be warned though, Friday and Saturday nights are generally heaving and despite lots of tables and chairs, it's usually standing room only. Those of a quieter disposition would be better off visiting mid-week.

Food includes homemade lasagne, cod and chips, bean, celery and coriander chilli and vegetable Kiev.

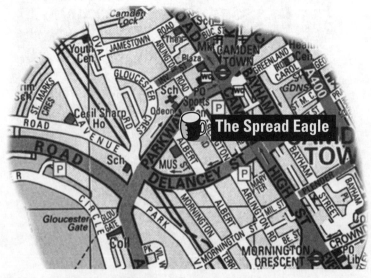

Quinns

65 Kentish Town Road

Open: Monday to Thursday: 11-midnight; Friday and Saturday: 11-1 and Sunday: 12-10.30

Food: Monday-Friday: 12-3 and 8-12; Saturday: 12-3 and 8-1 and Sunday: 12-4 and 8-10.30

❀ ☎

☎ 020 7267 8240

Camden Town tube and Camden Road rail

Beers: Greene King IPA and Abbot Ale, Adnams and Fuller's London Pride are available regularly. The pub also stocks around 50 different kinds of Belgian, French and German beers.

I have fond memories of the previous incarnation of this pub, although I can't remember what it was called. I was a student just around the corner and used to lavish most of my meagre grant behind its bar, in exchange for being allowed to be pretentious in charge of a pint. Well I was studying English. Anyway, things have moved on apace and now my old college is a posh pizza parlour, I still wax lyrical about a pint, but now get paid for it, and the pub is called Quinn's.

A free house, owned by the Quinn family – mom, dad and three sons – for more than a decade, this large, well-run, proper Irish pub still provides a welcoming place to wile away an hour or two. There's a long bar, comfortable sofa seating and the décor is a controversial mix of modern colour and Victorian design – a useful talking point if you run short of conversation. Its late license is something I would have heartily approved of, back in those days when I could make it past 10.30 without yawning. There's a fine range of well-tended ales and food includes chilli con carne, shepherd's pie and daily changing vegetarian dishes.

...also worth trying

Lansdowne

90 Gloucester Avenue (Chalk Farm tube)

This Primrose Hill Victorian corner pub regularly offers an interesting range of real ales but majors on its imaginative menu.

Queens

49 Regents Park Road (Chalk Farm tube)

Another gastro pub in Primrose Hill, complete with stripped floors, stylish furniture and beautiful listed stained glass windows.

NW3

Bull and Bush

North End Way, Hampstead

Open: Monday-Saturday: 12-11 and Sunday: 12-10.30
Food: Monday-Sunday: 12-10
& ❀ ❧ Ⓟ
☎ 020 8905 5456
Golders Green tube and bus 268
Beers: Bass, Tetley and Morland's Old Speckled Hen are available regularly. Fuller's London Pride is a guest.

"Come, come, come and make eyes at me, down at the Old Bull and Bush, " sang famous music hall star Florrie Ford in 1903 – and she was singing about this historic pub, which is opposite Golders Hill Park and on the edge of Hampstead Heath.

Originally a farmhouse, the earliest record of a license to sell ale dates back to 1721. Artist William Hogarth drank here, apparently taking time out from painting the Rake's Progress to do a spot of recreational gardening. Other notables who visited include Gainsborough, Reynolds, Garrick, Wilkie Collins, George Du Maurier and Dickens. In the Edwardian era the pub became a firm favourite with Cockneys on a day out to the 'country'. For those curious to find out more, there are boards around the pub detailing its history, lots of old photographs and even a free booklet to take home with you.

The present building was reconstructed in 1924. The pub has lots of alcoves, high back settles, three coal fires that are lit every day in winter and masses of old photographs of past music hall stars.

Food is a bit more interesting than the average, with highlights including beef and ale pie, salmon brouchette, cous cous with roasted winter vegetables served with an organic basil and tomato sauce, and spaghetti with olives and goats cheese.

Duke of Hamilton

23-25 New End, Hampstead

Open: Monday-Saturday: 12-11 and Sunday: 12-10.30
Food: Monday-Sunday: Sandwiches and rolls only
❀ ❧
☎ 020 7794 0258
Hampstead tube
Beers: Fuller's London Pride and ESB are available regularly. Guests might include Adnams and Cottage. There is also farmhouse cider on hand pump. Bottle-conditioned beers include Fuller's 1845 and Worthington White Shield.

This comfortable, 200-year old traditional free house relies on the quality of its beer to attract customers, who may include actors from the New End Theatre next door. And its pedigree is sound, as it has been in CAMRA's *Good Beer Guide* for the last nine years and, in 1997, was awarded the North London Pub of the Year award. Landlady Mary Wooderson is also the proud owner of a prestigious Cask Marque.

There's a terrace at the front and floral displays in summer. The walls feature sporting memorabilia that leans towards a cricketing bias. There are no machines or piped music and food is a simple menu of sandwiches and rolls.

The Freemasons Arms

32 Downshire Hill, Hampstead

Open: Monday-Saturday: 12-11 and Sunday: 12-10.30
Food: Monday-Saturday: 12-10; Sunday: 12-9
& ❀ ໖

☎ *020 7433 6811*

Hampstead and Belsize Park tube, Hampstead railway and buses 24, 116 and C11
Beers: Bass and Tetley are regularly available.

For those bored with the neon-lit, technological wizardry of modern bowling alleys, why not try the real thing? The Freemasons Arms has one of the last skittle alleys in the capital in its basement, ideal for placating fidgeting youngsters and their fed-up parents. And for those who've not quite had their fill of Hampstead Heath greenery, there is also a huge beer garden, which is divided into dining and drinking only areas.

Set back from the road and with a whitewashed exterior, this 1930s pub has wood paneling, high back settles and bow windows. Close by are the famous Hampstead Heath sights of Keats House, Kenwood House and Parliament Hill. Food includes beef and Bass ale pie, cod and chips and Three Shires sausage and mash. For vegetarians, the menu changes seasonally but might include Stilton, chestnut and stout bake or ratatouille.

The Magdala

2A South Hill Park, Hampstead

Open: Monday-Saturday: 11-11 and Sunday: 12-10.30
Food: Monday-Friday: 12-3 and 6.30-10; Saturday: 12-10; Sunday: 12-9.30
❀ ໖

☎ *020 7435 2503*

Belsize Park tube, Hampstead railway and buses 24, 46, 116 and C11
Beers: Greene King IPA and Fuller's London Pride are available regularly.

Although I suspect it will always be best known as the pub where Ruth Ellis shot her lover – and so gained her place in history by becoming the last woman to be hanged in Britain – the Magdala is also attempting to gain a reputation for the high standards of its food, which is cooked to order and uses only fresh produce.

For those interested in the macabre details of the former, you can still see the bullet holes in the wall outside and there is plaque commemorating the event.

Meanwhile foodies will be keen to know that options emerging from the open-fronted theatre style kitchen might include: lemon risotto with butternut squash, a large seafood selection that is fresh daily, steak and various pasta dishes.

The Spaniards

Spaniards Road, Hampstead

Open: Monday-Saturday: 11-11 and Sunday: 12-10.30
Food: 12-10 every day
❀ ☎ ℗
☎ *020 8731 6571*
Golders Green and Hampstead tube. Bus 210
Beers: *Dick Turpin's Ale (brewed by the Coach House brewery in Warrington) Bass and Fuller's London Pride are available regularly. There is one guest, which might include Bateman's, Smiles, Wychwood, Cottage, Hydes, Exmoor, Nethergate, Brain's or Oakhill.*

According to one of the many legends about this atmospheric and historic Hampstead Heath pub, notorious highwayman Dick Turpin was born here on September 21, 1705, when his father was the pub's landlord.

Allegedly, he was inspired to compel the rich to 'stand and deliver' after watching the antics of the visiting wealthy ladies and gentleman from an upstairs room. His horse Black Bess was reputedly stabled in the now listed tollhouse over the road.

Whether you're convinced of the tale or not, it provides a good excuse for a beer festival, which is held annually to commemorate Turpin's birthday and includes a dozen or so different real ales and entertainment for grown-ups and children.

Those of a more gentle nature may prefer to know that the pub also has a number of literary connections. Apparently the poet Keats was inspired to write Ode to a Nightingale whilst drinking in the garden and other visitors include Goldsmith and Byron. The pub is also mentioned in Charles Dicken's Pickwick Papers and Bram Stoker's Dracula.

Food might include seafood chowder, rosemary roasted lamb shanks, shepherd's pie with a spiced parsnip mash and a variety of salads.

...also worth trying

Flask

14 Flask Walk (Hampstead tube)
Not to be confused with the Highgate Flask, this Young's pub sits in a lovely alleyway just around the corner from the tube station.

Holly Bush

22 Holly Mount (Hampstead tube/railway)
Once the home of artist George Romney, the stables now form the back bar of this small historic pub, which has gas lamps outside.

NW8

The Clifton

96 Clifton Hill, St John's Wood

Open: Monday-Saturday: 11-11; Sunday: 12-10.30
Food: Monday-Saturday: 12-3.30 and 6.30-10; Sunday: 12-10
&. ☙
☎ 020 7602 3039
St John's Wood or Maida Vale tube and bus 139
Beers: Tetley's, Timothy Taylor's Landlord, Fuller's London Pride, Bass and Adnams are available regularly. Guests might include Adnams Broadside and Burton Ale.

The Clifton is the perfect pub for cricketing fans who like the Beatles, as it neighbours both Lord's Cricket Ground and Abbey Road.

Originally built as a house in 1837, it became a pub in 1894. There's a front garden and small rear patio, lots of wooden paneling and floors with rugs. Look out for the unusual Temperance Society mirror feature.

Rumour has it that King Edward VII spent many a happy hour here with the actress Lillie Langtry. Today's clientele may include a few actors and pop stars, as well as those seeking to drown their sorrows or celebrate the fate of their cricket team. And for those spectators unable to get into the ground, there is a television in one of the bars.

Food includes sausage and mash, cod, chips and mushy peas, steak and ale pie, cheese and broccoli bake and roasted vegetable lasagne.

Crockers Folly

24 Aberdeen Place, Maida Vale

Open: Monday-Saturday: 11-11; Sunday: 12-10.30
Food: Monday-Friday: 12-3 and 6-9; Saturday: 12-3 and 6-8; Sunday: 12-8
&. ❀ ☙ *in the dining room*
☎ *020 7286 6608*
Edgware Road or Warwick Avenue tube
Beers: Adnams, Greene King and Brakspear are available regularly. There's a varying choice of guest beers.

If you think that Crocker's Folly has all the splendour of a grand fin de siècle hotel, rather than a pub in an unprepossessing street in north west London, you would be right – for that was its original purpose.

Victorian speculator Frank Crocker was tipped the wink that a new railway station was to be built in Maida Vale. Believing that the development would enable him to make his fortune, he set to work to build the most opulent and elegant hotel imaginable, complete with marble columns, bar counters and walls, huge baronial marble fireplaces, intricately moulded ceilings and engraved glass windows. Opening in 1898, the Crown Hotel offered bars and restaurants on the ground floor and guest rooms above that were reached by sweeping, yes you guessed it, marble staircases.

Then came the devastating announcement: the station was not to be built over the road but a mile away, at Marylebone. Legend has it that poor old Crocker was so distraught that he jumped to his death from one of the rooms at the top of the hotel – but, although his lack of entrepreneurial skills certainly left him penniless, the reality is he lived to a ripe old age. Although it was colloquially known as Crocker's Folly for decades, the pub didn't officially change its name until the 1980s.

Although the flamboyant architecture provides entertainment enough, there's a pub quiz on Thursdays and live music and jazz on Saturday and Sunday. There's also bar billiards, darts, cribbage or chess. Food includes pie of the day – which might be steak and ale, fisherman's pie, chicken and mushroom and others – pasta of the day, for example, green pesto and olives, and fresh vegetable and noodle stir fry.

NW10

Grand Junction Arms

Acton Lane, Willesden

Open: Monday to Thursday: 11-11; Fri: 11-1; Saturday: 11-12; Sunday: 12-10.30
Food: Monday to Thursday: 12-9; Fri: 12-12.30; Saturday: 12-11.30; Sunday: 12-8
& ❀ ☞ *at weekends;* Ⓟ
☎ *020 8965 5670*

Harlesden rail and bus 260
Beers: All beers are from Young's brewery and include Bitter, Special and Triple A.

With moorings on the Grand Union Canal, a large garden and children's play area, this spacious Young's pub has three contrasting bars and offers live music on Friday and Saturday nights. Food is homemade and includes roast of the day, shepherd's pie, sausage and mash, vegetable curries, lasagne and quiche.

William IV

786 Harrow Road, Kensal Green

Open: Mon-Wednesday: 12-11; Thursday to Saturday: 12-12; Sunday: 12-10.30
Food: Monday-Friday: 12-3; Saturday: 12-4; Sunday: 12-4

&. ❀ ❤ Ⓟ

☎ *020 8969 5944*

Kensal Green tube and buses 18 and 52

Beers: Fuller's London Pride, Ruddles and Boddingtons are available regularly. Guests might include Charles Wells Bombardier, Trafalgar, Equinox and Black Adder.

Trendy real ale drinkers, who want to listen to the latest club sounds while supping a decent pint, will approve of this free house, where DJs play from Wednesday through to Saturday.

The pub décor also combines traditional and modern, featuring original fireplaces and wood paneling and floors, set amid mosaic tiling and a contemporary use of colour.

Food is top nosh and includes sirloin steak with tomato relish and chips, breast of chicken with pumpkin risotto, sea bass with shitake mushrooms, tagliatelle with roasted peppers, red onions and mozzarella and tortilla with spicy tomato sauce and rocket. They also provide a set two or three course Sunday lunch.

HARROW

The Castle

30 West Street, Harrow-on-the-Hill

Open: Monday-Saturday: 11-11; Sunday: 12-10.30
Food: Monday-Saturday: 12-3 and 6-9; Sunday: 12-4

&. ❀ ❤

☎ *020 8422 3155*

Harrow-on-the-Hill tube and buses H17 and 258

Beers: Fuller's London Pride and ESB.

Close to Harrow public school, the Castle is a traditional English pub, with no music or games machines, serving well tended Fuller's ales. Food includes sausage and mash, gammon, egg and chips and a full Sunday lunch, served with Yorkshire pudding.

PINNER

Queens Head

31 High Street, Pinner

Open: Monday-Saturday: 11-11; Sunday: 12-10.30
Food: Monday-Sunday: 12-2
❀ ⓟ
☎ *020 8868 4607*
Pinner tube
Beers: Adnams, Fuller's London Pride, Young's Special, Tetley and Greene King Abbot Ale *are available regularly.*

This Grade II listed, Tudor fronted pub is the oldest in Pinner. Parts of the building date back to 1540 and an alehouse is believed to have stood on the site since the first Pinner fair in 1336. The pub is in a picturesque street that is often featured in television programmes, including *Inspector Morse*, *Birds of a Feather* and *From May to September.*

There's no music or fruit machines, but those seeking entertainment can enter the pub quiz, held every Monday. Food includes a daily changing homemade pie, like beef and mushroom or chicken and ham, fresh fish on Friday, homemade soup, vegetable and leek bake and jacket potatoes.

STANMORE

The Malthouse

75 Stanmore Hill

Open: Mon-Tuesday: 4-11; Wednesday and Thursday: 4-12; Friday and Sat 11-1 and Sunday: 12-10.30
Food: None
♿ ❀ ☙
☎ *020 8420 7265*
Stanmore tube
Beers: Throughout the year there is a constantly changing list of real ales from more than 100 breweries.

A vibrant community pub, the dual emphasis at this free house is on well-kept and varied real ale originating from up to 100 breweries, enjoyed in friendly and entertaining surroundings.

There is a DJ and live music on Friday and Saturday evenings and, although there's no regular menu, free food is often provided as part of Saturday's theme night. Other entertainment includes a pub quiz on Tuesday and occasional music on Wednesday and Thursday.

For those keen to find out the pub's history, it's told in a series of photographs dotted around the walls.

ENFIELD

The Kings Head

Market Place, EN2

Open: *Monday-Saturday: 11-11; Sunday: 12-10.30*
Food: *Check with pub for times*
&*Partially;* ❀
☎ *020 8366 9381*
Enfield Town railway
Beers: *Tetley Bitter, Greene King IPA and Adnams are available regularly.*
The central market location, good cask ales, and high ratio of female to male customers ensures that the Kings Head provides a welcoming atmosphere. Built in 1899, a pub has stood on this site since the market was granted its charter by James I. There's a quiz every Tuesday and food includes home cooked roast gammon, broccoli and potato bake and traditional Sunday lunch.

The Old Wheatsheaf

3 Windmill Hill, EN2

Open: *Monday-Saturday: 11-11; Sunday: 12-10.30*
Food: *Monday to Saturday: 12-2*
❀ ☙ ℗
☎ *020 8363 0516*
Enfield Chase railway
Beers: *Tetley Bitter, Adnams Bitter and Broadside and Benskins are available regularly. Guests include Morland's Old Speckled Hen.*
This traditional two-bar friendly pub regularly wins awards for its floral displays and has been a local CAMRA Pub of the Year.

Just a minute's walk from Enfield Chase railway station, the present building dates from the turn-of-the-century, with an extension added in the 1930s. You can still spot the words 'Bottle and Jug' etched into the glass, a reminder of those days when pubs had a thriving take-home trade.

When we visited late on Saturday afternoon, everyone was gathered around the television in the lower bar catching the latest sports results, while the upper bar extension was quieter, with a few newspaper reading regulars, but perhaps a little less atmospheric. Food includes steak and kidney pie, fish and chips and jacket potatoes.

The Rose and Crown Tavern

Clay Hill, EN2

Open: Monday-Saturday: 11-11; Sunday: 12-10.30
Food: Monday to Sunday: 12-3
❀ ☎, until 6.30; Ⓟ
☎ 020 8366 0864
Enfield railway and bus 610
Beers: Courage Best and Greene King IPA.
With all the appearance of a country pub and backing onto Whitewebbs Golf Course, the Rose and Crown is one of Enfield's oldest hostelries, dating back to the 1700s.

It's also yet another pub that the infamous north London highwayman Dick Turpin is reputedly linked with, via his grandfather. Set on two floors and protected as a historic site by the National Trust, the inside features old oak beams and three open log fireplaces. There's live jazz and blues on Thursday, Friday and Saturday evenings and a quiz held every Tuesday. Food includes cod and chips, lasagne, ploughman's lunches, vegetable pasta bake and soup.

The Wonder

1 Batley Road, EN2

Open: Monday-Saturday: 11-11; Sunday: 12-10.30
Food: All day and every day.
♿ ❀ Ⓟ
☎ 020 8363 0202
Gordon Hill railway and bus 191
Beers: McMullen's AK is available regularly. Guest beers are drawn from the McMullen's Special Reserve range and feature McMullen's seasonal brews plus others from different breweries.
The owner of a prestigious Cask Marque, perhaps not surprisingly the Wonder boasts a higher than average turnover of cask ales.

A gabled Tudor-style exterior leads to two bars where you will find a lively range of entertainment on offer while you swig. This includes piano sing-a-longs every Wednesday, Friday and Sunday afternoon, plus Friday evening, and live music on Saturday and Sunday.

The home cooked food features a selection of Indian dishes – including vegetable biriani – jacket potatoes and pies.

BARNET

Hadley Hotel

113 Hadley Road, New Barnet, EN5

Open: Monday-Saturday: 11-11; Sunday: 12-10.30
Food: Monday-Saturday: 12-2.15
&. ❀ ℗
☎ 020 8441 0329
High Barnet tube station or New Barnet railway
Beers: Marston's Pedigree, Morland's Old Speckled Hen, Fuller's London Pride and Webster's Yorkshire Bitter are all available regularly.

After a stroll through Hadley Woods what better way to satiate your thirst than a pit stop at the comfortable Hadley Hotel. Hidden away in leafy suburbia, this traditional Victorian building stands on a corner plot with a garden attached, where children are welcome. The snug features a recently completed mural, depicting the Battle of Barnet. Food options include liver and bacon, home made chicken pie and various omelettes with chips or salad.

The King's Head

84 High Street, EN5

Open: Monday-Saturday: 11-11;
Sunday: 12-10.30
Food: Monday-Saturday: 12-2.30
&. ❀ ℗
☎ 020 8449 0645
High Barnet tube station
Beers: McMullen's AK Bitter.
The oldest site of a pub in
Barnet – there's been one here
since 1626 – the King's Head
is opposite St John the Baptist
Church. Reputedly it was the
first pub in the area to serve
drinks from glasses rather than

pewter pots. The usual pub fare of baguettes and jacket potatoes are supplemented with a daily special. There's live music monthly.

King William IV

18 Hadley Highstone, EN5

Open: Monday to Thursday: 11-3 and 5.30-11; Friday and Saturday: 11-11; Sunday: 12-10.30
Food: Monday: 12-2.15; Tuesday-Saturday: 12-2.15 and 7-10; Sunday: 12-4
❀ ☎ Ⓟ
☎ *020 8449 6728*
High Barnet tube and bus 84
Beers: Adnams, Greene King IPA, Burton's and Benskins are available regularly. There is also a house ale, Hadley Bitter, brewed by Ushers.

Close to the site of the Battle of Barnet and on the very edges of London, this is a 17th century traditional coaching house, with no music or gaming machines to spoil the peace and quiet. There's a new restaurant at the rear and food options include calves liver and bacon, Welsh rarebit with apple, home made steak and kidney pie, spaghetti arrabiatta and spinach and ricotta cannelloni.

The Lord Kitchener

49 East Barnet Road, New Barnet, EN4

Open: Monday-Saturday: 11-11; Sunday: 12-10.30
Food: Monday-Saturday: 12-2.30
❀ Ch: Only for food; Ⓟ
☎ *020 8449 3124*
New Barnet railway; Arnos Grove/Oakwood tube station
Beers: McMullen's AK Bitter is available regularly. Gladstone, Summertime, Harvest Moon and Castle are occasional guests.

A winner of a Cask Marque, this cosy well-furnished pub features the history of Lord Kitchener. There's a fish and chip quiz every Thursday evening and live music on alternate Saturdays. Food includes tuna and pasta bake, gammon steak and lasagne.

SOUTH LONDON

SE1

Anchor Tap

20A Horselydown Lane

Open: *Monday-Saturday: 11-11; Sunday: 12-10.30*
Food: *Monday-Saturday: 12-9 and Sunday: 12 until sold out*
❀ ☙
☎ 020 7403 4637
Tower Hill tube; London Bridge railway and buses 42, 78, 47, 188 and 381
Beers: *Samuel Smith Old Brewery Bitter*

This deceptively large mid 18th century River Thames pub was the first to be owned by John Courage when he bought the nearby Anchor Brewery in the 1790s. While the brewery has long since been turned into apartments, the pub has survived the onslaught of "progress" in more ways than one, for the Anchor Tap must be one of the few pubs left in the capital where you can sample a proper pint of Sam Smith's Old Brewery Bitter. A few years ago the Tadcaster brewery stopped selling real ale at many of their London outlets, replacing it with the sanitised plastic keg version – but thankfully it's the real McCoy here.

The Anchor Tap is a cosy, dark wood panelled, traditional pub with five interconnected warren-like rooms on the ground floor. These include a small well-appointed lounge, a room that's just big enough for a pool table and a separate games room, where a collection of beeping electronic zap games are housed in one place, enabling those of us desperate to avoid them to drink our pints in relative peace. There's also a small courtyard garden, which I suspect is a haven for those seeking shade on those rare days of sweltering city heat.

Food includes filled baguettes, burgers, vegetable Kiev and veggie lasagne. Entertainment is officially provided in the form of a pub quiz on Thursdays but there's also a resident playful ghost to spice things up a bit. Called Charlie, his favourite ruses include smashing all the ashtrays in the dead of night and fiddling with the volume control on the pub's sound system.

Step outside the pub, walk a few paces to the right and suddenly looming ahead is Tower Bridge in all its glory – a spectacular sight, particularly when lit at night, even for jaded ex city dwellers like me.

Founders Arms

52 Hopton Street, Blackfriars

Open: Monday-Saturday: 11-11; Sunday: 12-10.30
Food: Monday-Saturday: 12-8.30 and Sunday: 12-7
&. ❀
☎ *020 7922 1390*
Blackfriars tube and railway
Beers: *Young's Bitter, Special and Triple A. Guests beers include Young's Winter Warmer and Smiles.*

As estate agents advise, the three most important considerations when buying property are location, location and location – and, as the proud owners of the Founders Arms, Young's clearly took those words of wisdom to heart and must be laughing all the way to the bank.

When the brewery built the pub in the late 70s, they knew they were on to a sure winner, as the building enjoyed one of the finest panoramic views in the capital, facing St Paul's Cathedral across the river, with Canary Wharf blinking away in the distance. Indeed, Roger Protz used the vista from the pub as the front cover photograph for his CAMRA Best Pubs in London Guide, published in 1989.

As if that wasn't enough, life got even better for the Founders when Shakespeare's Globe Theatre was authentically reconstructed at a spot barely two minutes' walk away. And the icing on the cake arrived last year, when the much-acclaimed Tate Modern became their next-door-neighbour. Also nearby is the newly built but still wobbling Millennium Bridge, which the developers claim is a symbol of today's Britain – presumably their assertion is not based on the facts that it's expensive, shaky and, at the time of writing, closed until further notice.

While other pub critics appear to love the unapologetically modern design of this pub, personally I found it cold, uninviting and a bit like drinking in an upmarket student union bar. However, judging by the flurries of crowds it attracts, I think I'm probably the only person who holds this opinion. Certainly the views are breathtaking and the Founders has cleverly capitalised on its natural advantage with a wall of glass overlooking the river.

Food includes fresh haddock in Young's beer batter with fries, the ubiquitous sausage and mash and hot roasted lemon chicken baguette, while vegetarians can choose from options like mushroom and lentil cannelloni and roasted vegetables and sun dried tomato baguette.

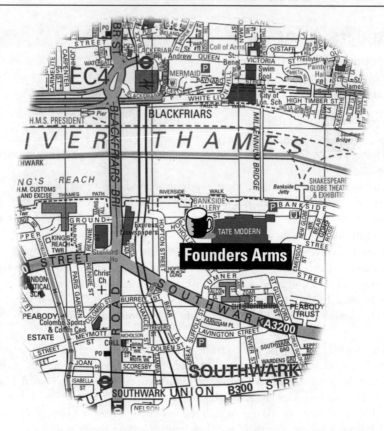

The George Inn

off 77 Borough High Street, Southwark

Open: Monday-Saturday: 11-11; Sunday: 12-10.30
Food: Monday-Friday: 12-4; Saturday and Sunday: 12-4. There's also a restaurant that is open from 12-2.15 Monday to Friday and 6-9.15 Monday to Saturday
✿ ⌖
☎ *020 7407 2056*
London Bridge tube and railway
Beers: Regulars are Boddingtons, Flowers, Fuller's London Pride, Morland's Old Speckled Hen, Greene King Abbot Ale and the pub's own Restoration Ale. Guest ales change weekly and might include beers from Bateman's or Wychwood.

Owned by the National Trust, this 16th century coaching inn, which was known to both Shakespeare and Dickens, can only be described as stunning and then some. Sodden in history, the George has stood on this spot since Elizabethan times, while the present building dates from 1677 and is the only remaining galleried inn in the capital.

Step through the small gateway that leads off Borough High Street and you leave behind the 21st century, including the increasingly common but unwelcome sight of bouncers standing guard at the door. Although polite and helpful, quite why they are necessary here is a mystery. Is it really likely that tourists will start hacking bits off to take home as souvenirs or scrawling graffiti across the historic walls? The pub comprises five low-ceilinged, lattice windowed rooms and my favourite is the first on the right as you walk across the courtyard. Called the Old Bar, it boasts a huge fireplace and such a slope that you feel drunk even before your first sip. Unfortunately this particular room is not always open to the public as it's available for private hire, and although there is an Old Curiosity Shop style glass fronted bar with a hatch, it remained firmly shut during our visit, leaving us with the minor irritation of having to face the cold December air outside and then nip back in again to the next bar along to get served – but it was worth it to avoid the piped music.

It would be easy to rest on its laurels and simply rely on its good looks and noble pedigree to get the punters flocking, but the George also takes its beer seriously, serving a varied array of well-kept brews, including Restoration Ale, brewed by the small local Bishops brewery. In addition, it plays host to occasional mini beer festivals. Food is standard pub fare and includes steak, mushroom and Guinness pie, sausage and mash, cod and chips, roasted vegetable lasagne and jacket potatoes.

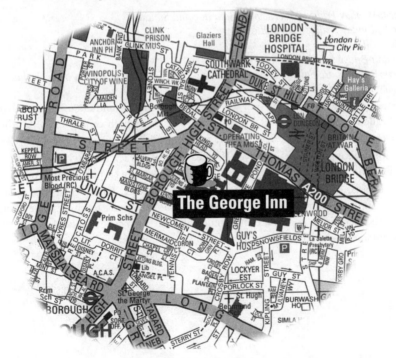

Kings Arms

25 Roupell Street, Waterloo

Open: Monday-Saturday: 11-11; Sunday: 12-10.30
Food: Monday-Friday: 12-3
❀ ☎ *until 6pm*
☎ 020 7207 0784
Waterloo tube and rail
Beers: Regulars include Adnams, Pedigree, Tetley and Ushers. There are four guest beers every month and these might include Brakspear's.

Well-kept beer and a courtyard conservatory that doubles as a restaurant are just two of the attractions of this Waterloo pub, that has made regular appearances in CAMRA's *Good Beer Guide*.

A grade II listed building, with two bars, wooden floors and open fires, it's also handy for both the National and Old Vic theatres. Chilli con carne, a variety of burgers including vegetable, Cumberland sausages and nut roast are some of the food choices available.

Leather Exchange

15 Leather Market Street

Open: Monday-Friday: 11-11; closed Saturday and Sunday
Food: Monday-Friday: 12-3 and 6-10
☎ 020 7407 0295
London Bridge tube and railway
Beers: Regulars are Fuller's London Pride and ESB. Seasonal and guest brews include Honey Dew, Red Fox and Jack Frost.

After a brief spell when the pub was leased by a juggling and circus co-operative and called the Juggler's Arms – perhaps they liked the high ceilings – the Leather Exchange reverted to its former name in the late 1990s.

Within walking distance of Tower Bridge, the real old leather exchange is just around the corner and Bermondsey antiques market is a stone's throw away.

There's a large room with a wooden floor and, for once, lots of chairs and tables to accommodate the busy lunchtime crowd. Those looking to satisfy their hunger may choose from a menu offering homemade burgers, various specialist sausages and mash, moules mariners or mushroom strogonoff and rice.

The Lord Clyde

27 Clennam Street

Open: Monday-Friday: 11-11; Saturday: 12-4 and 8-11; Sunday: 12-4 and 8-10.30
Food: Monday-Friday: 11-11; Sat and Sunday: 12-4

☎ *020 7407 3397*

Borough tube and London Bridge tube and railway
Beers: Regulars are Young's Bitter, Young's Special, Courage Best, Greene King IPA and Shepherd Neame's Spitfire. In winter, there's always a strong ale on offer.

"A proper local London boozer – a little gem" says the Lord Clyde's landlord, Michael Fitzpatrick, whose family has been running this pub since 1956. Michael and his wife Lucy took over the reins of this warm, inviting back street pub from his father in 1975, winning London licensee of the year in 1997.

Back in the 1980s, when I worked just around the corner, I was a regular customer, stopping off for a quick one after work and finding the welcome so warm that it was hard to wend my weary way back to dreary Borough tube station to face the long wait for the misery line. Indeed I celebrated – or commiserated – my redundancy here with the rest of my sacked mates, when the charity we worked for went belly up. There could be no finer place to contemplate the future which, in those salad days, encompassed little more than whose turn it was to get the next round in.

Thankfully some things never change. An inn has stood on the site for 300 years, while the current building dates back to 1913. Unspoiled, it features traditional pub décor, including lots of gleaming brass, etched mirrors, wood panelling and walls covered with historical prints and photographs.

Entertainment includes a monthly quiz night and darts board. There are a variety of well-kept beers to choose from and food includes homemade options like vegetarian quiche, steak and kidney pie, cheddar, Stilton and Brie jacket potato and salt beef sandwiches.

Tucked away in a tiny side street off Marshalsea Road, it's a little bit hard to find, but will handsomely repay your perseverance.

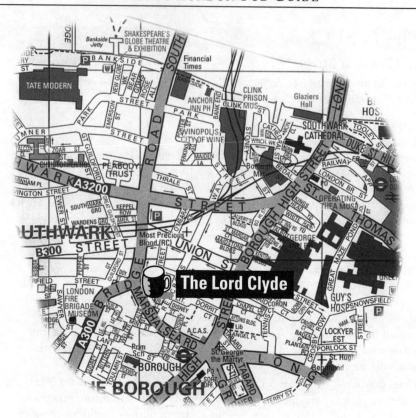

The Lord Clyde

The Mad Hatter

3-7 Stamford Street

Open: Monday-Saturday: 11-11; Sunday: 12-10.30
Food: Monday-Sunday: 12-9
&. ☎

☎ *020 7401 9222*

Southwark, Waterloo or Blackfriars tube

Beers: Regulars are Fuller's ESB, London Pride and Chiswick. Seasonals include organic Honey Dew, Summer Ale, Red Fox and Jack Frost.

This comfortable, tastefully appointed, upmarket pub has the feel of a hotel lobby, which is perhaps not surprising as there is a hotel attached. Sited on the south side of Blackfriars Bridge, the pub has wood panelling, green and gold walls, brass lamps, etched mirrors and glass and some fetching black and white tiling around the bar area.

The theme is as discrete as the décor, encapsulated in nine hats in glass cases dotted above the seating area facing the front entrance to the bar – blink and you'd probably miss them. There's a u-shaped bar and a large dining area towards the rear of the pub. As it's a Fuller's ale and pie house, the menu leans towards a pastry base with steak and ale, chicken spinach and bacon, a special "top hat" pie made with pork and stilton and red onion melt.

The Market Porter

9 Stoney Street, Borough Market

Open: Monday-Saturday: 11-11; Sunday: 12-10.30
Food: Monday-Sunday: 12-2.30
& Ch: weekends only
☎ 020 7407 2495
London Bridge tube and railway
Beers: Regulars are Harvey's and Courage Best. There are around 20 different guest ales each week, including porters, milds, summer ales etc.

Anyone who thinks real ale is on its last legs should be forced to visit the Market Porter. And it's hardly a punishment as the pub, with its open fires, wood panelling, barrels used as tables and cosy back room, is as warm and welcoming as any could be. The research for this guide has largely involved visiting as many pubs as I could in the limited time available. Very few managed to persuade me to stay for the luxury of a second pint, but I couldn't resist it in this one.

Although the pub is part of the small Market Taverns group, landlord Tony Heddigan has complete say in the beers on offer, enabling him to choose about 20 different ales each week. Often his choices feature innovative micro breweries or unusual beers. We sampled three from the Fisherrow Brewery – Seventy shillings, Eighty shillings and Freetraders – and voted them well-kept, interesting and definitely moreish.

As a result of his enterprising commitment to cask conditioned beer, 60 per cent of the pub's total beer sales are real ale – and if you don't believe the statistics, you can see the evidence all around you, as every table had someone on it drinking a pint or half of the proper stuff. The staff are helpful and friendly and although we developed hunger pangs five minutes after they officially stopped serving food, they kindly obliged us with a hearty snack.

Just as I've always believed, real ale attracts a diverse bunch of devotees and the pub's clientele reflects all walks of life. On a Saturday afternoon in December, there was everyone from the intriguing hippy couple in the corner, ploughing their way through what looked like six months' worth of old Sunday newspapers, to the upper crust gent keen to find out the rugby result and the young designer labelled blades laughing at my note-taking, perhaps assuming I was some sort of bizarre pedantic tourist who must keep notes of everywhere they went on holiday.

The area is interesting too as the pub faces Borough Market, open during the day at weekends, mostly selling vegetables, but from Monday to Friday functioning only at night. The aptly named pub is one of the few in London to have an early licence, offering breakfast and a pint from 6am. Food for the rest of the day includes sirloin steak, Cajun chicken, pasta, nut roast and lasagne. Personally I can't wait to make a return trip – but it's unlikely that I'll ever be one of their first customers of the day.

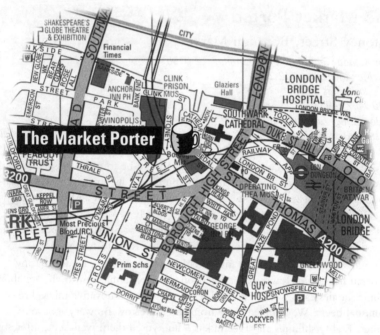

Old Thameside Inn

Pickford's Wharf, Clink Street, Southwark

Open: Monday-Saturday: 12-11 (winter) and 10-11 (summer); Sunday: 12-6 (winter) and 12-10.30 (summer)
Food: Monday-Friday: 12-4 and 5-8.30; Sat and Sunday: 12-4
♿ ❀ ☙
☎ *020 7403 4243*
London Bridge tube and railway
Beers: Regulars are Fuller's London Pride, Tetley, Bass and Adnams.
Call me old-fashioned, but running the gauntlet of more beeping gaming machines than the average amusement arcade, ear-splitting music and the over-powering smell of chips doesn't give me the impression I'm entering "London's

most famous riverside pub". If only the thumping base had been toned down and
the electronic wizardry removed to the other end of the bar, I might have been
tempted to stay longer, because the pub's in a pleasant location and could be an
ideal venue to wile away an hour or two after a spot of local sightseeing.

Originally an old tea warehouse, there's a drinking area overhanging the river and
berthed next door is the reconstruction of Sir Francis Drake's ship, the Golden
Hinde. Built in 1973, using traditional crafts and materials, it's now an educational
museum, offering school field trips and living history experiences, where youngsters can learn at first hand about life on board a Tudor warship and Drake's voy-
ages of discovery. There's even an option to stay overnight, so the pub must be
handy for those teachers who draw the longest straws and get the chance to nip
out for a quick pint. Also nearby is the Clink Museum, once the most famous
prison in the land, which could perhaps offer a lucrative line in alternative facilities for particularly naughty children.

Food includes bangers and mash, fish, chips and mushy peas, sandwiches, jacket
potatoes, vegetable curry, pasta dishes and spinach and mixed pepper tart.

The Royal Oak

44 Tabard Street

Open: Monday-Friday: 11-11; closed Saturday and Sunday
Food: Monday-Friday: 12-2.15 and 6-9.15
&

☎ *020 7357 7173*
Borough tube and bus 21
Beers: *All from Harvey's brewery. Regulars include Sussex Mild, Pale and Best. Guests
might include Armada, Kiss, Porter, Knots of May, Tom Paine, Southdown Harvest, Old
Ale, Bonfire Boy and Christmas Ale.*

This beautifully restored traditional Victorian two bar local is the Sussex brewer,
Harvey's only London pub. Just off Borough High Street, Tabard Street, formerly
Kent Street, was London's main road to Kent and the route of Chaucer's
Canterbury Pilgrims.

The street corner pub features a tiled exterior with large windows, wooden
floors, lots of chairs and tables and a dark red and cream colour scheme. To add to
the authenticity, there's no television, machines or canned music. Food too leans
towards the traditional and includes bangers and mash, cottage pie and steak and
kidney pudding. Indeed, my only quibble is why not open at the weekend?
While it's a little off the beaten track, it's a pleasant stroll from the many historic
attractions of Bankside and reasonably close to a tube station, so my bet is that it
would at least attract its fair share of thirsty, footsore sightseers. And it's the perfect
place to spend a tranquil, lazy Sunday afternoon reading the newspapers…

Shipwrights Arms

88 Tooley Street, Bermondsey

Open: Monday-Saturday: 11-11; Sunday: 12.10.30
Food: Monday-Friday: 12-2.30; Sat and Sunday: 12-4

ප

☎ *020 7378 1486*

London Bridge tube and railway

Beers: Regulars include Young's, Young's Special, Bass, Marston's Pedigree, Charles Wells Bombardier, Brakspear and Courage Directors.

This homely, unassuming pub seems to be losing most of the local competition to the redevelopers – we spotted at least two pubs within strolling distance already boarded up and waiting for the demolition men to arrive. Hopefully the female figurehead adorning the building outside will serve to protect them from any such threats.

Inside there's one big room with large windows, decorated in Christmas colours of bottle green and dark red, with a central bar and tables dotted around it. The lack of corners or cubicles to hide away in gives it a community feel, and you can imagine that it's a good venue for a knees-up. On the wall at the left is the 107 year-old pub's most striking feature – a tiled painting of shipwrights at work, dating from when the pub was first built. As the cheery bar maid told us: "You always panic when you give it a wipe in case one of the tiles falls off."

Food too is unpretentious and includes home made steak and kidney pie, sausage and mash, cod and chips, pasta and veggie kiev.

...also worth trying

Anchor

1 Bankside (London Bridge tube/rail)
Creakingly atmospheric, historic, riverside ale house, with half-a-dozen different rooms. Samuel Pepys is believed to have watched the Great Fire of London from here.

Wheatsheaf

6 Stoney Street (London Bridge tube/rail)
A regular in CAMRA's *Good Beer Guide*, serving a diverse and changing variety of ales. Opposite Borough Market and almost next door to the Market Porter.

SE3

The British Oak

109 Old Dover Road, Blackheath

Open: Monday-Saturday: 11-11; Sunday: 12-10.30
Food: Mon-Thurs: 12-9; F-Sunday: 12-7
❀ ☛ ℗
☎ 020 8858 1082
Blackheath, Westcombe Park or Charlton railway station
Beers: Courage Best and Directors and Greene King IPA are available regularly. Guest beers include Marston's Pedigree, Young's Special, Fuller's London Pride, Charles Wells Bombardier and Shepherd Neame Spitfire.

'Selling good beer to good people' is how the British Oak likes to describe itself.

This two bar comfortable pub, with its cast iron balcony at the front of the building, attracts a mixed and mostly local clientele of artists, musicians, teachers and pensioners. While the public bar has television and discrete music, there's neither in the saloon bar, allowing customers to focus their full attention on either playing on the bar billiards table or having a quiet chat. Other entertainment includes occasional jazz bands and talent nights.

Outside, there's a large patio area at the front and a walled patio at the rear with well-tended flowerbeds. Look out for the Morris dancers who may make a guest appearance in the summer. Picturesque Blackheath village and heath is 10 minutes walk away as is the top entrance to Greenwich Royal Park. Nearby is Blackheath RFC, which is apparently the oldest open rugby club in the world.

There's a changing list of guest beers, which the licensee hopes to expand on over the coming year. Food is incredibly cheap but cheerful, and includes pub grub stalwarts like fish and chips, steak and chips and steak and gravy pie.

SE6

Rutland Arms

55 Perry Hill, Catford

Open: *Monday-Saturday: 11-11;*
Sunday: 12-10.30
Food: *All day, every day*
✿
☎ *020 8291 9426*
Catford railway station
Beers: *Adnams Broadside, Bass,*
Fuller's London Pride and ESB
and Young's Bitter and Special
are all available regularly.
Worthington White Shield is also
available.

With five live jazz sessions a
week and assorted jazz memorabilia on the walls, it's not hard to guess where this
pub's heart lies. This is a large, L-shaped, one bar pub with lots of seating. Other
entertainment includes a pub quiz held once a month. Although there are no guest
beers, six real ales are regularly available. Food includes plaice, scampi, steak, stuffed
aubergine with red pepper sauce and vegetables en croute with a tomato sauce.

...also worth trying

Catford Ram

9 Winslade Way (Catford railway station)
Modernised and friendly local in Catford shopping centre serving excellent food.
It's close to Lewisham Theatre, home of Catford Beer Festival.

SE8

Dog and Bell

116 Prince Street, Deptford

Open: *Monday-Saturday: 11.45-11; Sunday: 12-10.30*
Food: *Monday-Friday: 12-2.30 and 6-9 – no food at weekends*
✿ ℗
☎ *020 8692 5664*

Deptford or New Cross railway station and buses 47, 188 and 199
Beers: *Fuller's London Pride and ESB are regularly available. Guest ales include Adnams, Nethergate, Wye Valley, Young's, Bateman's and others.*

A beer lover's refuge, with no blaring jukebox or beeping fruit machines to detract from the quiet enjoyment of a well cared for pint of ale. Such is the consistent quality of its cask-conditioned beers that this popular back street local has twice been voted South East CAMRA pub of the year and makes regular appearances in the *Good Beer Guide*. Whisky lovers should note that there's also a wide range of malts on offer.

There's a pub quiz every Sunday evening – now in its 11th year – and other entertainment is provided by traditional pub games like bar billiards, shove ha'penny and darts. Food is reasonably priced and includes steak pie and chips, sausage and mash, stuffed vine leaves, hummus and salad and pasta in a spicy tomato sauce.

SE10

Ashburnham Arms

25 Ashburnham Grove, Greenwich

Open: *Mon-6-11; Tuesday-Saturday: 12-3 and 6-11; Sunday: 12-3 and 7-10.30*
Food: *Lunchtimes: Tuesday-Sun; Evenings: Tuesday and Friday only*

☎ *020 8692 2007*
Greenwich railway and DLR
Beers: *Shepherd Neame Master Brew, Best and Spitfire are regularly available. A variety of seasonal ales from Shepherd Neame are also available.*

Built in the mid 19th century – with a conservatory added in 1995 – this Shepherd Neame local has won a cabinet full of awards from both the brewery and CAMRA, encompassing the quality of its food, wine and of course, its all-important beer. A former CAMRA local pub of the year and regular entrant in the *Good Beer Guide* for the last decade, in 1997 the Ashburnham Arms won the brewery's best community pub accolade.

Although it's tucked away in a quiet residential street, it's also just a short stroll away from Greenwich's many historical sites – including the Cutty Sark, National Maritime Museum and the Royal Observatory. Back at the pub the attractions include a quiz night held every Tuesday, with a pop music quiz held on the last Tuesday of every month.

Food-wise, the speciality of the house is pasta dishes and eight different ones are regularly available, including vegetarian alternatives. But if pasta isn't for you, other options include sandwiches, baguettes and jacket potatoes.

Plume of Feathers

19 Park Vista, Greenwich

Open: *Monday-Friday: 12-11; Saturday: 11-11; Sunday: 12-10.30*
Food: *Monday-Fridayri: 12-10; Saturday: 11-10; Sunday: 12-4*
  ⚒ ❀ ☡
☎ *020 8858 0819*
Maze Hill railway
Beers: *Adnams Best and Webster's Yorkshire Bitter are available regularly. Guests might include Fuller's Jack Frost and others.*

Sitting on the Meridian Line overlooking Greenwich Park, the Plume of Feathers was built more than 300 years ago and is Greenwich's oldest pub. A traditional venue with good beer and a welcoming atmosphere, it also boasts a walled garden that's ideal for children. Food includes sirloin steak with all the trimmings, fresh lamb fillets, vegetable balti, fish and chips and various salads.

Richard I

52-54 Royal Hill, Greenwich

Open: *Monday-Saturday: 11-11; Sunday: 12-10.30*
Food: *Monday-Saturday: 12-230 and 6-10; Sunday: 12-2.30 and 6-9.30*
❀ *Ch: Only in the garden*
☎ *020 8692 2996*
Greenwich railway
Beers: *Young's Best, Special and Triple A are regularly available. Seasonal ales are also from Young's brewery.*

Not far from the heart of Greenwich, the Richard I is described by the publican as 'how pubs looked like in the 1950s'. This busy Young's pub is split into two different drinking areas, served by one bar. There's a large beer garden at the back, popular in the summer months. The regularly changing menu might feature fish and chips, pasta, shepherd's pie and Cajun chicken.

SE16

The Blacksmith's Arms

257 Rotherhithe Street, Rotherhithe

Open: Monday-Saturday: 12-11; Sunday: 12-10.30
Food: Tuesday-Saturday: 6.30-9.30; Sunday: 12.30-5
& ❀

☎ 020 7237 1349

Canada Water, Surrey Quays or Rotherhithe tube and bus 225
Beers: *Fuller's ESB and London Pride and Adnams are regularly available. Seasonal ales are from Fuller's brewery.*

Known locally as 'the village inn', this friendly Fuller's pub tends to be a popular focal point for many of Rotherhithe's newer residents.

The mock Tudor exterior, decorated with window boxes and hanging baskets in the summer, leads to a wood panelled interior featuring paraphernalia associated with the blacksmith's trade mixed with old local photographs. There's a games room where you can play pool or darts and a pretty walled garden towards the pub's rear. Other entertainment includes a pub quiz in the winter and occasional live music in the summer.

The bar menu features homemade burgers, steak and onion sandwiches on ciabatta bread, goat's cheese tartlets with tomatoes and black olives and aubergine and roast pepper mille feuille. There's also an upstairs restaurant, with a varying and eclectic menu that might include crispy belly of pork with apple and shallots, sea bass with fennel en papillote and oriental style duck served on a bed of noodles.

The Mayflower

117 Rotherhithe Street, Rotherhithe Village

Open: Monday-Saturday: 12-11; Sunday: 12-10.30
Food: Tuesday-Fri: 12-3 and 6.30-9; Sunday: 12-4
& ❀

☎ 020 7237 4088

Canada Water or Rotherhithe tube
Beers: *Greene King IPA, Abbot Ale and Morland's Old Speckled Hen are available regularly. There are various guest beers which change every two days or so.*

A must on every American tourist's itinerary, the Mayflower stands on the riverside near the spot where the founding fathers first set sail four centuries ago on their voyage of discovery to the New World.

Originally built in the 16th century then rebuilt two centuries later, the upper floor – which today houses the restaurant – was blown to pieces by a doodlebug during the blitz of World War II and was rebuilt in the 1950s. The black and white exterior, with its leaded windows, leads to an interior featuring the history of the ship and those who sailed in her, including a model of the Mayflower and other ships of the period, ships' lamps and old ships' timbers. There are creaking wooden floors and wooden settles in the small wood panelled rooms that are joined by narrow passageways. Outside is a small jetty overlooking the Thames offering spectacular views of the City.

Opposite the pub is the church of St Mary the Virgin, designed by Christopher Wren, where the captain and part owner of the Mayflower, Christopher Jones is buried, alongside two of his partners, John Moore and Richard Gardener.

Apparently the church's vicar is happy to give interested visitors an informal history lesson. And should you feel the sudden urge to write a postcard, you're in the right place, as the pub is the only one in London that also doubles as a post office, selling both British and USA stamps.

A Greene King pub, the Suffolk brews are joined by a changing list of guest ales that feature more unusual choices, like O'Hanlons and Rebellion. Food includes sausage and mash, liver and bacon, steak and Abbot pie (made with the beer, not an ecclesiastic), roasted vegetable pancake and aubergine and mozzarella bake.

Spice Island

163 Rotherhithe Street, Rotherhithe

Open: Monday-Saturday: 11-11; Sunday: 12-10.30
Food: Monday-Saturday: 12-10; Sunday: 12-9
 ♿ ❀ ☡ ⓟ
☎ *020 7394 7108*
Rotherhithe tube
Beers: Boddingtons, Flowers Original and Morland's Old Speckled Hen are available regularly.

From wallowing in history to unashamedly embracing all that is 21st century, Spice Island is a large, three-story, modern, converted warehouse. Its huge riverside terrace, heated in winter, boasts great views and guarantees this venue's popularity with tourists and trendy locals alike. All the big sporting occasions are shown on television and there's a DJ on Fridays, with dancing until midnight.

Food includes steak and mushroom pie, poached salmon, chicken fajita, vegetable Kiev, pasta bake and vegetable Wellington.

SE19

The Railway Bell

14 Cawnpore Street, Norwood

Open: Monday-Saturday: 12-11; Sunday: 12-10.30
Food: Monday-Friday: 12-3 and 5-8; Saturday: 12-3; Sunday: 1-5
❀ ☙ *until 7pm;* ℗
☎ *020 8670 2844*
Gipsy Hill railway
Beers: Young's Best, Special and Triple A are regularly available. Seasonal ales are also from Young's brewery.

Tucked away in a back street two minutes from the local station, the Railway Bell won first prize in a national competition for its own recipe 'Thai Taste Explosions' and its patio garden is also award winning.

A mid-Victorian detached pub, it retains some of its original features including two working fireplaces. There's a quiz every Tuesday evening, regular seasonal themed party nights – its Halloween and Bonfire party has achieved local renown – and, for those who prefer the grape to the grain, organised wine tastings. Other food includes traditional roasts, fajitas, sesame coated vegetable spring rolls and mushroom stroganoff.

SE22

The Clockhouse

196A Peckham Rye

Open: Monday-Saturday: 11-11;
Sunday: 12-10.30
Food: Monday-Friday: 12-10.30;
Saturday: 10-10.30; Sunday: 10-
10
♿ ❀ *Ch: Only outside or for*
meals
☎ *020 8693 2901*
East Dulwich railway and buses
12, 63 and 312
Beers: Young's Best, Special and
Triple A are regularly available.
Seasonal ales are also from
Young's brewery.

'I lost track of the time' would be a most unlikely excuse for returning home late after a visit to this pub, as you'll find yourself surrounded by it.

This otherwise traditional Victorian building features a clock in its peaked roof, while inside there's a plethora of timepieces, many of them unusual, heralding the passing of the hours with ticks, chimes and even cuckoos. Overlooking Peckham Rye Common, this Young's pub has won innumerable awards for its floral displays, including the prestigious London in Bloom accolade. For those with an aversion to cask breathers, note that the landlord occasionally uses one on the Triple A and other seasonal brews.

There's a quiz night on Tuesday and modern jazz on Wednesday. Food includes freshly made pizzas, homemade pies, traditional Sunday roasts, vegetable Wellington and stuffed mushrooms.

SE25

The Alliance

91 High Street, South Norwood

Open: *Monday-Saturday: 11-11; Sunday: 12-10.30*
Food: *Monday-Friday: 12-2*
&

☎ *020 8653 3604*

Norwood Junction railway and buses 75, 157, 196, 197, 312, 410

Beers: *Courage Best, Greene King Abbot Ale and Shepherd Neame Spitfire are regularly available. Occasional guest ales might include Wadworth 6X, Marston's Pedigree and Courage Directors.*

Built in 1860, the Alliance is a country-style pub, with leaded windows, beams and lots of brass jugs and pots hanging from the ceiling and the bar. Close to the station, with a long narrow bar and a friendly welcome, the consistent quality of its beer is recognised by its inclusion in CAMRA's *Good Beer Guide*. Food is only available weekday lunchtimes and includes grilled gammon, Cornish pasties, jacket potatoes and vegetable pasta bake. The pub may close on Saturday afternoons if local football team, Crystal Palace, is playing at home.

Portmanor Free House

Open: Monday-Saturday: 11-11; Sunday: 12-10.30
Food: Monday-Friday: 12-3 and 5-9.30; Saturday: 12-9.30 and Sunday: 12-7
✿ ☡
☎ 020 8655 1308
Norwood Junction and bus 165
Beers: Fuller's London Pride, Courage Best and Greene King Abbot Ale. *Guest ales might include those from the Hogs Back brewery and others.*

This is a well-established and popular free house, with an adventurous guest ale policy, often featuring choices from small microbreweries. There's a quiz on Thursday nights and a disco on Friday, Saturday and Sunday. Food includes steak and ale pie, sirloin steak, scampi and chips, vegetable burgers and lasagne.

SE26

Dulwich Wood House

39 Sydenham Hill

Open: Monday-Saturday: 11-11; Sunday: 12-10.30
Food: Mon- Sunday: 12-2.30
✿ ☡ *Only in the garden;* ℗
☎ 020 8693 5666
Sydenham Hill railway and buses 63 and 202
Beers: Young's Best, Special and Triple A are regularly available. Seasonal ales are also from Young's brewery.

Judging by the number of nominations the 'Woodie' received from CAMRA members, it appears to have achieved something of a cult following amongst those south of the river who know a well-kept pint when they find it. As one said: "My personal nomination for top London hostelry definitely goes to this pub – long may it continue to offer this regular a slice of perfection in south London!"

The striking building, featuring a short tower, was designed by Sir Joseph Paxton, the architect of the original Crystal Palace, and built in 1857. There's a secluded and well-landscaped garden where you can try your hand at boules while the children go off to play in their special area. The largely regular clientele is a mix of age, gender, occupation and interests – in recent times the pub has supported a cricket club, darts teams, a football team and a golf society. The pub also hosts a live jazz duo on Sunday evening and a monthly quiz.

A Young's pub, publican Peter Henderson wins praise from all-comers for the way his beer is kept in tip-top condition. Food includes cod in lager batter, sirloin steak, vegetable lasagne and a range of baguettes and ciabatta rolls.

SE27

...also worth trying

The Hope

49 Northwood High Street, West Norwood (West Norwood railway)
This friendly corner local is one of Young's longest held pubs.

BEXLEYHEATH

Robin Hood and Little John

78 Lion Road

Open: Monday-Friday: 11-3 and 5.30-11; Saturday: 11-3.30 and 7-11; Sunday: 12-4 and 7-10.30
Food: Monday-Saturday: 12-2.30
& ❀ ☙
☎ *020 8303 1128*
Bexleyheath railway
Beers: Fuller's London Pride, Shepherd Neame Spitfire, Courage Best, Brakspear Bitter and Harvey's are amongst the ales regularly available.

The opportunity to sample eight well-kept real ales is one of the attractions of this friendly back-street local, voted local CAMRA branch's pub of the year in 2000. Old sewing machines provide the tables in this otherwise traditional English pub, where the food includes steak, vegetable pasta dishes and sausage in French bread.

BROMLEY

...also worth trying

The Red Lion

10 North Road (Bromley North/South railway)
This back-street, friendly local provides two guest ales that change up to three times each week and may include choices from less well-known breweries.

BROMLEY COMMON

Two Doves

37 Oakley Road

Open: Monday-Friday: 12-3 and 5.30-11; Saturday: 12-3 and 6-11; Sunday: 12-3 and 7-10.30
Food: Monday-Sunday: 12-3
  ᕕ ✿ ᕐ
☎ *020 8462 1627*
Bromley South and Hayes and bus 320
Beers: Young's and Courage beers are regularly available and there is an ever-changing selection of real ales.

Over the last 12 months, this relaxed and homely Victorian pub on the edge of Bromley Common has offered more than 300 real ales from all over the British Isles. The local CAMRA branch pub of the year for 2000, it's in easy reach of the H.G. Well's Centre in Bromley and Charles Darwin House in Downe. The basic menu includes rolls and toasted sandwiches, salads and ploughman's lunches.

...also worth trying

Bird in Hand

62 Graves Road (Bromley South railway)
A comfortable back-street local's pub with a country theme, serving three real ales that might include Harvey's, Charles Wells Bombardier or Shepherd Neame Spitfire.

CHISLEHURST

The Bull's Head Hotel

Royal Parade

Open: Monday-Saturday: 11-11; Sunday: 12-10.30
Food: Monday to Thursday: 12-3 and 6-9; Fri-Sunday: 12-3. There is also a restaurant, open Monday-Saturday: 12-2.30 and 6.30-9; Sunday: 12-3.30
  ᕕ ✿ ᕐ Ⓟ
☎ *020 8467 1727*
Chislehurst railway
Beers: Young's, Bitter Special and Triple A are regularly available.

You'll find this spacious and comfortable Young's pub – with a small, three-star hotel attached – about a mile away from the local railway station. There are three main bars, including a quiet lounge bar, a brasserie and ballroom. Food includes fillet steak, steak and kidney pudding, leek and Camembert parcels and Thai green vegetable curry. The Chislehurst caves are a local tourist attraction and also nearby are Scadbury nature reserve and Brands Hatch motor racing circuit.

CROYDON

Dog and Bull

24 Surrey Street

Open: Monday-Saturday: 11-11; Sunday: 12-10.30
Food: Monday-Sunday: 12-2.30
& ❀
☎ *020 8667 9718*
East or West Croydon railway
Beers: Young's, Bitter Special and Triple A are regularly available. Seasonal ales also come from Young's brewery.
Visited by Prince Charles in 1995, this traditional Grade II listed ale house, with its award-winning large garden, is the oldest pub in Croydon and is set in the town's thriving street market. A past local CAMRA branch pub of the year, two drinking areas lead off from an island bar. Food is homemade and includes steak and kidney pie, curries, bangers – made with Special bitter – and mash and vegetable pasta bake. A pub quiz is held every Tuesday evening.

FOOTSCRAY

...also worth trying

Seven Stars

Footscray High Street (Sidcup railway)
A listed building dating back to 1600 and retaining some original features, the Seven Stars has weekly live music and a monthly quiz. Food is homemade and comes in large portions and the beers available might include Bass, Greene King IPA and Adnams.

SIDCUP

...also worth trying

The Alma

10 Alma Road (Sidcup railway)
A popular back-street old-fashioned local, serving at least three real ales that might include Shepherd Neame Spitfire or Young's Special. A pub quiz is held every Monday.

SOUTH CROYDON

Rail View

188 Selsdon Road

Open: Monday-Saturday: 11-11; Sunday: 12-10.30
Food: Monday-Fridayri: 12-3; Saturday: Only rolls available; Sunday: 1-4
& ❀ ➳ ℗
☎ *020 8688 2315*
South Croydon railway
Beers: Adnams Best, Hancock's HB, Fuller's London Pride, and Young's Special are available regularly. The guest beer changes each week.
This typical Victorian two-room local offers a friendly welcome and serves four real ales plus a guest beer that changes every week. Décor features a collection of railway paintings and there's a large garden. Daily homemade food specials might include beef and ale pie, sirloin steak or vegetable lasagne. A pub quiz is held every Sunday evening and dominoes or cribbage is played in the public bar.

SW1

Buckingham Arms

62 Petty France

Open: Monday-Friday: 11-12; Saturday: 12-11; Sunday: 12-5.30
Food: Monday-Saturday: 12-2.30 and 6-9; Sunday: 12-2.30
& ➳*, weekends only*
☎ *020 7222 3386*
St James Park tube and Victoria railway

129

Beers: *All beers are from Young's brewery and include Bitter, Special and Triple. Winter Warmer is available from October to March.*

If you're ever stuck waiting for your passport to be renewed, you may find yourself adjourning to the Buckingham Arms – and there could be far worse places to seek solace from form-filling bureaucracy than here.

As you might have guessed, this traditional Victorian pub is next door to the London Passport Office, but also close to the sights of Parliament Square – Westminster Abbey, Big Ben and the Houses of Parliament. However, for lovers of real ale it has a much more important claim to fame: it's one of only a handful of pubs to have appeared in every edition of CAMRA's *Good Beer Guide*.

Weekdays in the long mirrored bar attract a clientele of largely office workers, business people and civil servants with a scattering of tourists, while at weekends visitors to the capital take centre stage. Food includes 'The Mighty Buckingham Burger' – a homemade quarter-pounder – Camembert in breadcrumbs with hot redcurrant jelly, beef or vegetarian nachos, ploughman's lunches and toasted sandwiches.

Cask and Glass

39-41 Palace Street, Victoria

Open: *Monday-Friday: 11-11; Saturday: 11-3 and 6-11; Sunday: 12-3*
Food: *Monday-Friday: 12-3; Saturday: 12-2.30*
❀

☎ *020 7834 7630*
Victoria tube
Beers: *Shepherd Neame's Master Brew, Best and Spitfire are all available regularly.*

Despite – or perhaps because – we were two of only three women drinking in the Cask and Glass when we visited, we felt very at home here. And it's as well we did, as it's smaller than your average living room.

Landlord John Bernard says he's served two prime ministers and several MPs during his time running what is reputedly the second smallest pub in London. Just like politics, there's a few hard fought for seats, but more often than not standing room only to sip your choice of well-kept Shepherd Neame brews and admire the model aircraft dotted around. Food is sensibly kept to a minimum, with seven varieties of sandwiches, including vegetarian options, and hot sausages.

Fox and Hounds

29 Passmore Street

Open: *Monday-Friday: 12-3 and 5.30-11; Saturday: 12-3 and 6-11; Sunday: 12-3 and 6.30-10.30*
Food: *Monday-Friday: 12-2.30 and 5.30-8*
♿ ❀

☎ *020 7730 6367*
Sloane Square tube
Beers: *All beers are from Young's brewery and include Bitter, Special and Triple A.*

For those who share Oscar Wilde's opinion of fox hunting, this may not be the best choice of pub, particularly when you notice the stuffed fox, whose head is protruding from one side of a wall while its tail is poking out the other.

However, providing you face the opposite direction, away from both Basil Brush and the horrible Changing Rooms style makeover at the pub's rear, this tiny street corner local becomes a much more pleasant venue, with no music or gaming machines.

A traditional frontage leads to a cosy bar, with stripped floorboards, a few prints and a real fireplace. But look beyond to what must have once been the back room, and it appears that Handy Andy and his team of amateur decorators was let loose, as everything is either covered in MDF or has been subjected to a paint effect. Sit still for long enough and you're likely to find yourself the next victim of the runaway rag roller.

Until a year ago, this was the last 'beer only' pub left in the capital, but now they have a small range of spirits in addition to the well-kept Young's ales. Two minutes walk from Sloane Square tube, locals include Chelsea pensioners and the odd would-be thespian. Food is only available on weekdays and includes crispy bacon and avocado salad, vegetarian pasta of the day and bangers and mash.

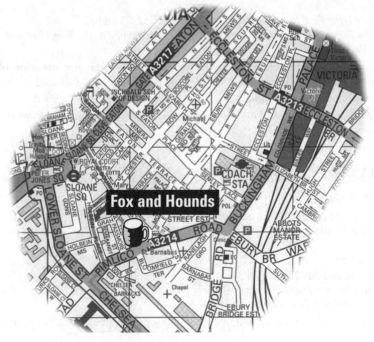

Golden Lion

25 King Street

Open: *Monday-Friday: 12-11; closed Saturday and Sunday*
Food: *Monday-Friday: 12-2.30*

❀ ☎

☎ *020 7925 0007*

Green Park tube

Beers: *Tetley, Greene King IPA, Adnams, Fuller's London Pride and Timothy Taylor's Landlord are all available regularly.*

Directly opposite Christie's auction rooms, the Golden Lion has been awarded a London Heritage Inn plaque. Built at the turn of the last century, the décor features beautiful leaded lights. There's always a good range of beers on tap plus occasional guests. Food includes fish and chips, pie of the day, steak sandwich, vegetable lasagne and vegetable curry.

Grouse and Claret

14-15 Little Chester Street

Open: *Monday-Friday: 11-11; closed Saturday and Sunday*
Food: *Monday-Friday: 12-2.30*

☎

☎ *020 7235 3438*

Victoria or Hyde Park tube and buses 2, 8, 16, 36, 38, 52, 73 and 82

Beers: *The Badger Brewery range such as Badger Best, Champion Ale, Tanglefoot and Sussex Ale.*

Excellent beer from the Dorset-based Badger brewery is the major attraction of this comfortable, dark wood-paneled Belgravia pub, which has a ground floor and cellar bar. Food options include Cumberland sausage, rib of beef, stuffed aubergines or tomatoes, and cauliflower cheese. The pub is only open at weekends to pre-booked parties.

Morpeth Arms

58 Millbank

Open: *Monday-Saturday: 11-11; Sunday: 12-10.30*
Food: *Monday-Saturday: 12-7; Sun 12-3*

♿ ❀

☎ *020 7834 6442*

Pimlico tube and bus 77A

Beers: *Regulars are from the Young's Brewery and include Bitter, Special, Triple A. Winter Warmer is available from October to March.*

While modern day architects might seek to design pubs with as small a space for the bar as possible, ensuring that the maximum number of punters can be crammed in, there's none of that nonsense at the Morpeth Arms.

The two-tier oak bar is huge and dominating, taking up half the room, and must be a joy to work behind. Built in 1845 and now a Grade II listed building, other notable features include dark wood paneling, lots of engraved glass and ornate plasterwork. Apparently – although for reasons that will become clear, I can't personally vouch for this – there is a particularly lovely oval stained glass window in the Gents.

Judging by the photographs, the Queen Mother and Prince Charles look like they might occasionally nip in for a quick snifter – closely followed by the world's press – while the rest of the clientele is made up of locals, tourists, the occasional MP and those who work in nearby MI5 and MI6.

Despite the secret service links, it's a friendly place and the lack of music seems to encourage conversation. We got chatting to a chap called Gordon from Aberdeen, who was fascinated by our note taking and wanted to know what we were up to. A reluctant lager drinker, who was baffled by the choice of real ales, we left just as he was about to buy his first pint of Winter Warmer.

Food includes steak and Guinness pie, a selection of fried fish, macaroni cheese, vegetable chilli and lasagne.

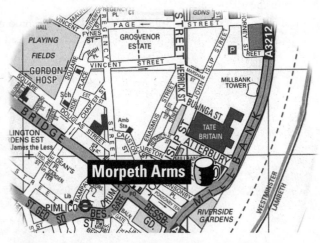

Nag's Head

53 Kinnerton Street, off Wilton Place

Open: Monday-Saturday: 11-11; Sunday: 12-10.30
Food: Monday-Saturday: 11-9; Sunday: 12-9
⌗ until 6.30
☎ 020 7235 1135
Knightsbridge tube
Beers: Adnams is always available. Occasional guests might include Fuller's London Pride.

Thank God I don't live near to the Nag's Head. Firstly I'd have to fork out about a million pounds a week for my mortgage and secondly, a similar amount would be owed on my bar bill, as I can't imagine I'd willingly miss a day's drinking in this wonderful, tiny mews pub that is easily one of my favourites in London.

Owned by retired actor Kevin Moran, it's the only free house left in this part of the capital. There are two rooms, the front has a small real fire and wooden floor while the back, reached down a few stairs, has a flag-stoned floor and larger open fireplace. Both are served by a diminutive sunken bar in the centre that barely reaches mid-thigh height and features the smallest bar stools I've ever seen. The beer engine is Victorian and was originally made for the Great Exhibition and the pumps have original Chelsea pottery handles.

The oak-paneled walls are adorned with all kinds of memorabilia, including cartoons depicting some of the local famous and infamous characters, old newspaper clippings and signed photographs of the household names who regularly join the locals to try to bag one of the 40 or so seats here. A card from television cook Clarissa Dickson Wright declares: "No longer barred – hurrah!" – a cause for celebration indeed. Against the walls are various Victorian entertainment machines, including a working 'What the Butler Saw' peepshow. To complete the atmosphere, music is from the 1930s.

Food includes real ale sausages, Brie or Stilton salad, steak and mushroom pie and Mediterranean vegetable quiche. Just like its soundtrack, the Nag's Head is a guaranteed classic.

Orange Brewery

37-39 Pimlico Road

Open: Monday-Saturday: 11-11;
Sunday: 12-10.30
Food: All day and every day
  , until 6pm, if eating
☎ 020 7730 5984
Sloane Square
Beers: All ales are brewed in the
micro-brewery on site and regulars are SW1, SW2 and Pimlico
Porter. There is usually a seasonal
ale, also brewed on site.

With its frenzy of blackboards
and predominantly young
clientele, you'd expect the
Orange Brewery pub to be playing something a little more contemporary than
crooner Glen Campbell. But then it was Saturday afternoon and laid-back music
seems to be the order of the day here, with traditional sing-alongs centred around
the piano a regular highlight.

For those wondering where the name derives from, the 18th century building was
once the Orange Coffee House and was dedicated to Prince William of the
House of Orange, who lived in Pimlico for a while. There are high ceilings,
stripped floors and open fires but undoubtedly the major draw is the beer, which
is all brewed on site at the pub's micro brewery. Those keen to find out more
about how it's done might want to take advantage of a brewery tour.

We tried SW1 and Pimlico Porter. The former chestnut-coloured brew was
hoppy and fruity with a slightly smoky aftertaste, which made it interesting, if
slightly too distinctive to be a session beer. The porter was lovely – sweet and
chocolatey, but perhaps a little too thin to appease the taste buds of reformed
Guinness drinkers, lured by its colour to try it. There's a bottle plant being
installed soon and for those who develop a taste for their ales, the pub offers four-
pint containers to take home.

Food is standard pub grub but reasonably priced for the area and served all day
and every day. Options include sausage and mash, steak, kidney and barley wine
pie and a veggie bean burger.

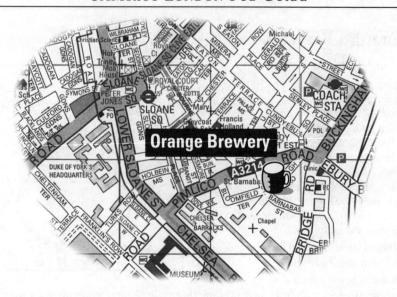

Red Lion

48 Parliament Street

Open: *Monday-Saturday: 11-11; Sunday: 12-7*
Food: *Monday-Sunday: 12-3*
♣
☎ *020 7930 5826*
Westminster tube
Beers: *Tetley is always available.*

If the prime minister had a local, this would be it. Barely a few minutes walk away from Downing Street, not surprisingly the largely male clientele leans heavily towards parliamentarians and their associated hangers-on, including lobbyists. There's even a division bell, summoning MPs to vote in the nearby House of Commons. Food includes steak and kidney pie, fish and chips, shepherd's pie and lasagne.

The Sanctuary

33 Tothill Street, Westminster

Open: *Monday-Saturday: 11-11; Sunday: 12-10.30*
Food: *Monday-Sunday: 12-9*
♿ 🐾
☎ *020 7799 4044*
St James Park tube and buses 211, 11 and 24

Beers: Fuller's London Pride, ESB and Chiswick are always available. Seasonal beers are from Fuller's and include Summer Ale, Red Fox and Jack Frost.

Not the posh Covent Garden health spa, frequented by frazzled females, but a spacious Fuller's Ale and Pie House, attached to a small hotel. As the Cask Marque award and inclusion in CAMRA's *Good Beer Guide* prove, the beer is in tip-top condition in this light and airy themed bar. Food includes Steak and ESB pie, fish and chips and two vegetarian choices that change daily.

The Stage Door

3 Allington Street

Open: Monday-Saturday: 11-11; Sunday: 12-10.30
Food: All day and every day
☕ *until 5pm*
☎ *020 7834 7055*
Victoria tube and bus 73
Beers: Greene King Abbot Ale and Morland's Old Speckled Hen are available regularly. Guest and seasonal beers include Smiles, Ushers, Bateman's, Caledonian, Brakspear, Wychwood, Thwaites and Hydes.

As you might guess from the name, the Stage Door is at the side of the Victoria Palace Theatre and near to the Apollo Victoria and so attracts a theatrical crowd, including some members of the cast of local shows.

Although it's one large room, with a bar facing the entrance, the alcove seating and dim lighting manages to engender a cosy atmosphere. A T&J Bernard Ale House, it follows their usual theme of bare floorboards and wooden paneling. There's a good range of constantly changing ales. Food includes fish, various pies, red pepper lasagne and veggie burgers.

Star Tavern

6 Belgrade Mews West

Open: Monday-Friday: 11.30-11; Saturday: 11.30-3 and 6.30-11; Sunday: 12-3 and 7-10.30
Food: Monday-Friday: 12-2.30 and 6-9; Saturday: 12-2.30 and 6.30-9 and Sunday: 12-2.30 and 7-9
☕
☎ *020 7235 3019*
Knightsbridge tube
Beers: All beers come from Fuller's brewery and include London Pride, ESB and Chiswick. There is one seasonal ale.

If stars were given for cleanliness, the sparkling Star Tavern would merit the maximum.

Included in every edition of CAMRA's *Good Beer Guide* and the winner of CAMRA's West London Pub 2000, this is a traditional, old-fashioned, friendly and extremely well cared for pub in a cobbled mews.

The bar is on the right as you walk in and there's a large room off to the left, featuring two real fireplaces. There's a predominantly green colour theme, a few prints, some padded bench seats against the walls and lots of other wooden seating and tables. Even the rather lurid carpet doesn't detract from the pub's home-from-home feel, which is mercifully unhampered by music, television or gaming machines. Upstairs is a second lounge, complete with its own small bar.

Food too veers towards the homely, with sausage, cod or chicken Kiev and chips, pasta dishes and vegetarian quiche regularly appearing on the menu.

White Swan

14 Vauxhall Bridge Road

Open: Monday-Saturday: 11-11; Sunday: 12-10.30
Food: Monday-Saturday: 12-9.30; Sunday: 12-9
&. ※
☎ *020 7821 8568*
Pimlico tube and buses 2 and 36
Beers: Courage Best and Directors, Theakston's Best Bitter and Greene King Abbot Ale are available regularly. There are usually two guest beers a week and these might include Everards, Nethergate, Wychwood, Gale's, Bateman's and Shepherd Neame.

Another T&J Bernard House, the White Swan is just around the corner from the Tate Gallery – that's the old one, not the Tate Modern – and so attracts more than its fair share of tourists. Thankfully it's large enough to comfortably accommodate all comers. Décor includes bare floorboards, lots of pale wood and plenty of wooden seating, including a raised seating area at the rear.

While it offers an impressive range of beers, unfortunately on the day we visited the service was painfully slow. Food includes beer battered fish and chips, Yorkshire pudding filled with roast beef, Theakston sausages, red pepper lasagne and salmon pasta melt.

...also worth trying

Westminster Arms

9 Storey's Gate, Westminster (Westminster tube)
While chairs may be in short supply, fortunately decent beer isn't in this rather barn-like pub that attracts many MPs and the occasional Chelsea pensioner.

SW3

The Australian

29 Milner Street, Chelsea

Open: Monday-Saturday: 11-11; Sunday: 12-10.30
Food: Monday-Saturday: 12-3 and 6-9; Sunday: 12-3
  ♿ ❀ ☡
☎ *020 7589 6027*
Sloane Square tube
Beers: Tetley's, Adnams, Pedigree, Greene King IPA and Abbot Ale are all available regularly.

The name is a reminder that the first England versus Australia cricket match was played just down the road in Lennox Gardens. Streets around the pub are also named after some of the players.

On the day we visited, the fascination with all things sporty was alive and kicking, as most of the pub's clientele was gathered around the television to watch the England versus Wales rugby tie. Although there was lots of loud banter and noisy cheering, it was possible to see that this ivy-clad pub has all the makings of a pleasant place to spend an hour or two.

The walls are half wood panelled, there's a central copper topped bar, wooden tables, padded bench seats and attractive wrought iron chandeliers. As you might expect, there's lots of pictures with a cricketing theme and other paraphernalia associated with the game. But the memories are not solely sporting: there's also a touching plaque above one of the seats at the pub's rear, commemorating the spot where a gentleman proposed to his intended. Let's hope that their marriage has fared better over the years than the varied fortunes of England's test cricketers.

To satisfy those for whom watching physical exertion inspires only hunger, food includes toasted pastrami and mozzarella sandwich, steak and kidney pie, warm honey chicken salad, ricotta and aubergine terrine and stuffed peppers with wild rice.

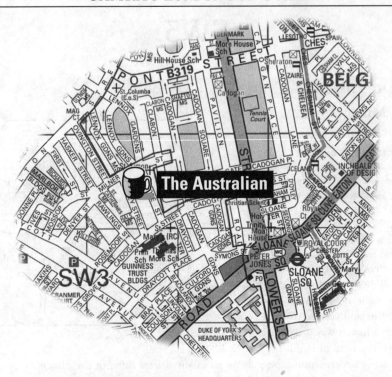

Bunch of Grapes

207 Brompton Road, Knightsbridge

Open: Monday-Saturday: 11-11; Sunday: 12-10.30
Food: Monday-Saturday: 11-10; Sunday: 12-10
♿ 👞
☎ *020 7589 4944*
Knightsbridge or South Kensington tube
Beers: *Courage Best and Directors are available regularly. Theakston's Old Peculiar is a guest.*

The Bunch of Grapes provides a welcome respite for those who've worn out their credit cards shopping at Harrods nearby. Although there's been a pub on the site since 1770, this incarnation was built in 1844. There's a central bar, lots of dark wood panelling and hand carved wood, and an attractive, large bow fronted window. Food includes fish and chips, sausage and mash, an assortment of pies, vegetable Stilton crumble and roast pepper lasagne.

The Cooper's Arms

87 Flood Street, Chelsea

Open: Monday-Saturday: 11-11; Sunday: 12-10.30
Food: Monday-Saturday: 12.30-3 and 6-10; Sunday: 12.30-3
&
☎ *020 7376 3120*
Sloane Square tube and buses 11, 19, 22 and 211
Beers: Young's Bitter, Special and Triple A.
The large windows enhance the bright and lively atmosphere of this street corner Young's pub. Close to the King's Road and Albert Bridge, there's a popular function room upstairs where, should you be lucky enough to have 24 friends, they can all dine at the same table. Food includes roast Mediterranean vegetables with cous cous and feta, pan fried fillet of sea bass, traditional Sunday roasts and spinach and ricotta tortellini in a tomato and basil sauce.

Moore Arms

61–63 Cadogan Street, Chelsea

Open: Monday-Saturday: 12-11; Sunday: 12-10.30
Food: Monday-Saturday: 12-3
& ❀
☎ *020 7589 7848*
Sloane Square tube
Beers: Wadworth 6X, Friary Meux, Burton Ale, Benskins and Greene King Abbot Ale are available regularly.
A regular winner in the Brighter Kensington and Chelsea floral competitions, the Moore Arms attracts a young and buzzing crowd. For the hungry, food options are likely to include soup of the day, burgers, fish and chips, vegetable chilli and mushroom stroganoff.

The Phene Arms

9 Phene Street, Chelsea

Open: Monday-Saturday: 11-11; Sunday: 12-10.30
Food: Monday-Friday: 12-3 and 6-10; Sat and Sunday: 12-4 and 6-10
& ❀ *Ch: Only in the garden*
☎ *020 7352 3294*
Sloane Square or South Kensington tube
Beers: Adnams Bitter and Broadside, Morland's Old Speckled Hen, Courage Directors and Best and Fuller's London Pride are all available regularly. Wadworth 6X and Charles Wells Bombardier are occasional guests.
Apparently, when George Best was known to be rather partial to the odd sherry,

this corner local was one of his favourite watering holes. Although he's now strictly under doctor's orders to stick to the lemonade, the Phene Arms doesn't lack for star quality, with the likes of Madonna, her hubby Guy Richie and actor Michael Angelis queuing up to take the places of former visitors, like Elizabeth Taylor and Ingrid Bergman.

The attraction is simple: it might be in the heart of trendy and ridiculously expensive Chelsea, but the Phene Arms offers all the conviviality and bonhomie of a small village pub, complete with beery, friendly locals, an excellent landlord and landlady and a cracking atmosphere, devoid of any pretension.

The black and white frontage, with an attached small patio garden, leads into the one-roomed 150 year-old pub, which features an island bar, lots of seating and large windows. There's some wooden cladding, carpets, a brick fireplace and fringed lampshades, adding to the overall impression that you're sitting in someone's slightly worn, but very comfortable living room. It's the kind of pub that would inspire you to go on marches, to protect it from the antics of those seeking to distress the walls, add contemporary lighting and, in the process, sanitise the ambience.

Food includes beer battered cod and chips, homemade burgers, fillet or sirloin of beef, halloumi salad with char grilled vegetables and a platter featuring red pepper, hummus, artichokes and olives. There's also a fine array of competitively priced sandwiches and rolls, all served with salad.

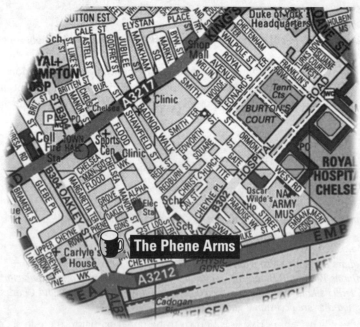

SW4

Bread and Roses

68 Clapham Manor Street, Clapham

Open: Monday-Saturday: 11-11;
Sunday: 12-10.30
Food: Monday-Friday: 12-3 and
6.30-9.30; Sat and Sunday: 1-4.30
and 6-10

☎ 020 7720 0140

*Clapham Common tube and
Clapham High Street railway;
buses 35, 37, 55, 88 and 365*
Beers: Adnams and Smiles are
available regularly. Occasional
guest beers vary.

Tory party leader William
Hague may want everyone to believe that he enjoys the odd pint of bitter or 14,
but he's one of the people you are least likely to bump into at this Clapham
venue, as the pub is owned by the Workers Beer Company and all the profits are
ploughed back into an assortment of trade union backed campaigns.

The name comes from a poem written by James Oppenheim in 1912, which was
later set to music. The lyrics, which I've always felt would make a fine epitaph,
say: "Our lives shall not be sweated from birth until life closes, Hearts starve as
well as bodies; Give us bread, but give us roses."

Meanwhile the Workers Beer Company will be familiar to those of us who spent
a large percentage of our youth rocking for or against something or another at
various outdoor pop festivals, as they're the ones organising the all-important pro-
vision of the drinks. An army may run on its stomach, but well-intentioned hip-
pies need ale and plenty of it.

But if you're expecting a crusty, leaking old tent and a queue for the toilets until
next Thursday, think again, because this is a much more stylish venue. The pub is
a modern bar, painted in bright pastel colours, set within a Victorian building.
There's a busy function room that hosts weekly comedy and music sessions and a
glass-walled terrace leading to the garden. Sunday afternoons are a big family
event, with African music, food, DJs and a children's arts workshop, all free. Food
includes sausages, Thai salad, pasta and vegetarian noodle dishes.

Rose and Crown

2 The Polygon, Clapham Old Town

Open: *Monday-Saturday: 11.30-11; Sunday: 12-10.30*
Food: *Monday to Thursday: 12-3 and 7-9; Fri: 12-3; Saturday: 12-4 and Sunday: 12-5*
✿
☎ *020 7720 8265*
Clapham Common tube
Beers: *Greene King IPA and Morland's Old Speckled Hen are available regularly. In addition there are three guest beers that vary.*

The Rose and Crown is justifiably proud of its commitment to cask ales, selling around half-a-dozen different guest beers from independent and regional breweries every week – adding up to more than 270 kinds during the last two years.

A Georgian house that was converted to a pub in 1892, there are low ceilings and the L-shaped bar area is divided by pillars and wood partitions. A small pub with a loyal following, it also does its bit to boost the coffers of local charities, hosting regular quiz and race nights. Food includes steak and kidney pie, tandoori vegetable masala and roasted Mediterranean pancake.

Windmill on the Common

Clapham Common Southside

Open: *Monday-Saturday: 11-11; Sunday: 12-10.30*
Food: *Monday-Friday: 12-10; Sat and Sunday: 12-9*
 ♿ ✿ ☂ ℗
☎ *020 8673 4578*
Clapham Common tube
Beers: *Young's Bitter, Special and Triple A are available regularly. Seasonal beers also come from Young's brewery.*

Built on the site of the home of the founder of Young's brewery, this pub offers very swish accommodation for those to whom money is no object – or their company is footing the bill.

The pub itself has several tastefully decorated rooms, including a conservatory and high domed lounge area, with open fires, comfortable seating, wood paneled walls and prints, lots of them featuring windmills. As it's directly on the Common and has seating outside, it's an excellent hotspot in the summer.

Food includes fine steak and ale pie, chicken satay and Young's beer battered cod. Vegetarian dishes change daily but might include vegetable stir-fry and stuffed aubergines.

...also worth trying

Manor Arms

128 Clapham High Street, Clapham (Clapham North/Common tube)
This is a traditional local pub, with a friendly welcome, serving well-kept beers that usually include Marston's Pedigree and Wadworth's 6X.

SW5

The Blackbird

Earls Court Road

Open: Monday-Saturday: 11-11; Sunday: 12-10.30
Food: Monday-Sunday: 12-9
☎ *020 7835 1855*
Earls Court tube
Beers: Fuller's Chiswick, London Pride and ESB are available regularly. Seasonal ales include Fuller's Jack Frost, Red Fox, Summer Ale and Honey Dew.
A former bank, now this is a Fuller's 'Ale and Pie House', catering for local residents as well as visitors to the nearby exhibition centre. Although 'Blackbird pie' features on the menu, it's made with sausage and bacon rather than our feathered friends. Food options also include bangers and mash, fish and chips, vegetarian chilli and potato skins with mushrooms.

SW6

The Duke of Cumberland

235 New Kings Road, Fulham

Open: Monday-Saturday: 11-11; Sunday: 12-10.30
Food: Monday-Friday: 12-2.30 and 7-9; Saturday: 12-2.30 and Sunday: 1-3.30
❀ ➤
☎ *020 7736 2777*
Parsons Green tube and bus 21
Beers: All from Young's brewery, including Bitter, Special and Triple A.
Although we were warned by one of the chatty locals to stay well away when Chelsea FC was playing at home, it was hard to imagine that the Duke of Cumberland could be anything other than a very pleasant, relaxing and friendly place to enjoy a pint of well cared for Young's beer.

Built in 1863, there's a high ceiling complimented by large leaded and stained glass windows, giving the pub a light and airy feel even in the midst of winter. Décor includes bare floorboards, a large bar surrounded by pillars with a huge brass chandelier over the top, and lots of mismatched chairs and tables. One wall is completely dominated by one of the finest pieces of ornamental tiling I've seen in a pub – for those keen to know these things, apparently it's a Fulham Potteries first edition.

The former rear public bar has been knocked through and, as there seemed to be some sort of children's party in full swing on the day we visited, we didn't venture further. One word of warning: the news from our regular was that the pub is due to undergo a refurbishment, so let's hope it's tackled sensitively.

Food is served in hunger-busting portions and includes specialist sausages, various meat dishes and a special daily vegetarian option.

Eight Bells

89 Fulham High Street

Open: *Monday-Saturday: 11-11; Sunday: 12-10.30*
Food: *Monday-Saturday: 11-3*
 ♿ ❀ ★
☎ *020 7736 6307*
Putney Bridge tube and buses 14, 22, 220 and 85
Beers: *Shepherd Neame Spitfire and Courage Best are regularly available.*

Reputedly the oldest pub in Fulham, the Eight Bells is a cosy local, barely a couple of minutes walk from the tube station, and attracting everyone from young baseball capped lads on their way to the football match to old dears out for a chin-wag.

Decorated like someone's slightly shabby but snug parlour, there's wooden cladding, carpets, fresh flowers dotted around, a few prints, decorative plates and a grandfather clock. Seating is on carved wooden settles at old tables in this one room pub, which has a small horseshoe shaped bar with a food servery at the side. There are daily specials, including tuna steak with fresh vegetables, and the usual burgers, jacket potatoes and lasagne. A new addition is a wood fired oven, enabling authentic pizzas to be produced.

Imperial

577 King's Road

Open: *Monday-Saturday: 12-11; Sunday: 12-10.30*
Food: *Monday-Friday: 12-2.30 and 7-9.30; Sat and Sunday: 12-3.30*
 ♿ ❀
☎ *020 7736 8549*
Fulham Broadway tube and buses 11 and 22
Beers: *Haggard's Imperial Bitter; Charles Wells Bombardier.*

Despite the unmissable bright blue exterior, we still managed to walk straight past the Imperial. Perhaps it's because it looks less like a pub and more like a cool bar – even the pub sign is given a modern-day twist in metal.

Contemporary it may be, but there's still real ale. Indeed the pub sells beer produced by the owners, Andrew and Tim Haggard, at their brewery in Battersea. Food is more interesting than most with options including wild boar sausages, served with bubble and squeak, warm goat's cheese salad, and penne with courgettes, olives and mushrooms with a tomato and basil sauce.

The White Horse

1-3 Parson's Green, Fulham

Open: Monday-Saturday: 11-11; Sunday: 12-10.30
Food: Monday-Friday: 12-3 and 5.30-10; Sat and Sunday: 11-10
& ❀ ☙
☎ 020 7736 2115
Parson's Green tube and buses 14 and 22
Beers: Adnams Broadside, Harvey's Sussex Best, Highgate Dark Mild, Rooster's Ranger, Rooster's Yankee and Bass are all available regularly. Guest beers are available at a quarterly beer festival, including the annual old ale festival, which features around 50 or so old ales, porters and barley wines. Bottled beers include all the trappist ales plus around 40 or so others from around the world.

I so wanted to love this pub. It seems that everyone but everyone applauds its bright and airy décor, its high-class gastro pub style food – deemed worthy of a star in Susan Nowak's Good Pub Food – and its clear commitment to good beer by, for example, hosting regular ale festivals that showcase unusual choices. So why do I feel unable to join in singing its praises?

We arrived at around mid-day on Saturday and already things were hotting up for the lunchtime trade, to the extent that there was a bit of a scrum to find a vacant table. We were just about to sit down with our halves of Rooster's Ranger, when a member of staff appeared, unceremoniously pointing to another area at the back and barking that we should remove ourselves there. Meanwhile our chairs were snaffled for a couple who had arrived later, but were about to eat. It was hard to recover from feeling like second-class citizens. Had we wanted to eat, food options include truffled mushroom risotto, beer battered fish and chips, chargrilled ribeye steak and Lancashire cheese and caramelized onion tart.

And then there's the clientele. It's not that I demand whippets, flat caps and a nice pint of mild to feel at home, but they're certainly an improvement on the massed ranks of Barbour jackets, four-wheel drives and elegantly coiffed gels lounging around on sofas, drinking designer water. In essence, it seems to be a pub for those who don't like them much – which perhaps explains why I was destined for disappointment…

SW7

Anglesea Arms

15 Selwood Terrace

Open: *Monday-Saturday: 11-11; Sunday: 12-10.30*
Food: *Monday-Friday: 12-3 and 6.30-9.30; Sat and Sunday: 12-9.*
& ❀ ☡
☎ *020 7373 7960*
South Kensington and Gloucester Road tube and buses 74 and 14
Beers: *Adnams, Brakspear, Fuller's and Greene King are available regularly. Guest beers might include Hook Norton, Young's Winter Warmer, Bateman's, Harvey's and Fuller's Summer Ale.*

Genuine oil paintings on the mahogany paneled walls, real ale, really good food and the odd bona fide celebrity are the hallmarks of the Anglesea Arms. There are no games machines or music and, although there is a television, soccer fans should note that it's only switched on for international rugby, cricket and tennis fixtures. Food includes bangers and mash with onion or mustard gravy, crab cakes and salad, homemade pie of the day, traditional roast on Sunday and grilled vegetables with goats cheese.

SW8

The Priory Arms

83 Landsdowne Way, Stockwell

Open: *Monday-Saturday: 11-11; Sunday: 12-10.30*
Food: *Monday-Saturday: 12-2.30; Sunday: 12.30-3.30*
❀
☎ *020 7622 1884*
Stockwell tube
Beers: *Adnams Bitter and Broadside and Harvey's Best are available regularly. Guest beers vary.*

Local CAMRA members believe the Priory to be the best free house 'for miles around', voting it their south-west London pub of the year on almost too many occasions to list.

A Grade II listed building with large windows, it has a wooden floor and some carpeting, light coloured walls and bench seating. Three well-kept regular ales are joined by a changing menu of different beers from microbreweries – some 3, 000 have been offered to date. In addition there's a fine array of German bottled beers, including smoked, wheat, alt and dunkel. Indeed the pub hosts a German beer festival in October. Fruit wines are also available.

Entertainment includes a free pub quiz on Sunday evening and there are board games for the bored. Food includes a renowned Sunday lunch, sausages and mash, quiche, scampi, nut Wellington and at least four daily specials.

Royal Albert

43 St Stephen's Terrace

Open: Monday-Saturday: 12-11; Sunday: 12-10.30
Food: Monday-Friday: 12-2 and 7-10; Saturday: 1-3; Sunday: 1-5.30
& ❀ Ch: Only in the beer garden
☎ *020 7735 8095*
Oval or Stockwell tube
Beers: Flowers Original, Fuller's London Pride, Boddingtons, Wadworth 6X and Adnams are available regularly. Guest ales include Bateman's, Jennings, Hop Back, Everards and Rebellion.

A quarter-of-a-mile away from the Oval cricket ground, the Royal Albert has a definite competitive streak. Bar billiards and pool are played here, there's a twice a week quiz on Tuesdays and Sundays, board games are available, all sports are shown on the large screen television and, to cap it all, they tune in daily to both 15 to 1 and Countdown!

A former dance hall, décor features two open fires and five chesterfield sofas. The bar has a bare wooden floor while there are carpets in the two snugs and the pub's mini library, tucked away at the pub's rear. Outside is a beer garden, with a boules pitch. Other entertainment includes a jazz club on alternate Thursdays and a monthly comedy evening. Food includes steak and ale pie, Sunday roast, spinach and feta goujons, vegetable chilli and lasagne.

...also worth trying

Mawbey Arms

7 Mawbey Street, South Lambeth (Vauxhall tube)
This is a cosy, well-furnished pub, with a garden, serving Shepherd Neame ales. Lambeth Palace is nearby.

Surprise

16, Southville (Stockwell tube)
Next to Larkhall Park, this Young's pub was a 'beer only' house until the 1950s. Given its long-standing commitment to serving well-kept ale, it's perhaps not surprising that the Surprise is a stalwart *Good Beer Guide* entrant. Décor features some interesting caricatures of regulars past and present.

SW9

The Landor

70 Landor Road, Clapham North

Open: Monday-Saturday: 12-11; Sunday: 12-10.30
Food: Tuesday-Saturday: 6-9; Sunday: 1-6
❀ ⛄

☎ *020 7274 4386*

Clapham North tube

Beers: *Shepherd Neame's Spitfire and Greene King IPA are available regularly. Guests include Young's Special, Bass, Morland's Old Speckled Hen, Marston's Pedigree and others.*

The fates have turned for pub fringe theatre. Where once every London pub with its own tiny theatre seemed only too keen to swap it for a restaurant or extra seating, thankfully now most seem to see them as an attraction rather than a hindrance.

And the Landor is no exception. Its own thriving fringe theatre opened in 1994, seats 40 to 50 and offers a diverse programme from various small theatre companies, including the next-door-neighbours from the famous Italia-Conti drama school. How many other pubs have their own regular supply of budding luvvies on the doorstep?

The pub itself has had a relatively recent 'refurb', which includes the addition of some sailing paraphernalia on the ceiling. There's a beer garden outside and the beer is looked after well enough to merit inclusion in CAMRA's *Good Beer Guide*. For those who prefer to play an active role in their entertainment, there's a pub quiz every two weeks. Food includes organic sausages and mash, chicken curry, vegetable curry and vegetarian shepherd's pie.

...also worth trying

Trinity Arms

45 Trinity Gardens (Brixton tube)
Built in 1850, the Trinity Arms is a quiet retreat, serving well-tended Young's beers, within a few hundred yards of Brixton's busy town centre.

SW10

The Chelsea Ram

32 Burnaby Street

Open: Monday-Saturday: 11-11; Sunday: 12-10.30
Food: Monday-Saturday: 12.30-3 and 7-10; Sunday: 12-3 and 7-10
&. ❀ ☎
☎ *020 7351 4001*
Sloane Square or Fulham Broadway tube and buses 11 and 22
Beers: The Young's range, including Bitter and Special.

Perhaps it's licensee Nick Elliot's insistence that children are welcome in his pub, providing they're 'on leads!' but certainly, during our visit, while several families were in evidence, the younger members were on their best behaviour. Maybe it's the promise of some of the pub's lip smackingly lovely food, which was awarded a star by Susan Nowak in CAMRA's Good Pub Food. The changing menu might include such delights as pumpkin and ginger soup, pea and ham risotto, cod served with baby vegetables or Chelsea Ram salad.

The yellow and green colour scheme, large arched windows and glass roof extension ensure that, even on the gloomiest of winter days, the pub's atmosphere remains sunny and cheerful. The Chelsea Ram is also to be congratulated for cleverly managing to combine many of the qualities of a street corner local – a television, friendly bar staff, jocular bar-propping regulars and well-kept beer – with those of a more upmarket venue – posh nosh and an ad hoc art gallery, where you can buy the paintings displayed on the walls. It's a rare and welcome feat.

SW11

The Castle

115 Battersea High Street, Battersea

Open: Monday-Saturday: 12-11; Sunday: 12-10.30
Food: Monday-Saturday: 12-3 and 7-9.45; Sunday: 12-9.30
&. ❀ ☎ *at weekends;* ℗
☎ *020 7228 8181*
Clapham Junction railway
Beers: Young's Bitter, Special and Triple A. Seasonal beers are all from Young's brewery.

Built in 1965, even the publican says it's 'extremely ugly' outside but if you expect the same story inside, you're in for a pleasant surprise. The interior has been tastefully refurbished to look like a warm, spacious and modern café-bar-cum-pub, with a conservatory and tables and chairs outside in the summer.

The convivial atmosphere is enhanced by small touches like offering daily news-papers and having a children's room on Sundays. And although it may have the feel of a bar-restaurant, the licensees are proud of their high turnover of Young's ales. Their commitment to looking after them to a consistently high standard is reflected in their inclusion in CAMRA's *Good Beer Guide*. For those who prefer other forms of intoxication, there's a varied and reasonably priced wine list and what the publican promises is 'the best cappuccino in town'.

Food is good enough to be favourably remarked upon in various food guides and the Observer newspaper. Typical English staples – like sausage and mash and steak and kidney pie – are joined with other more exotic dishes whose roots lie in French, Spanish, Greek, North African or Asian cooking.

The Latchmere

503 Battersea Park Road, Battersea

Open: Monday-Saturday: 12-11; Sunday: 12-10.30
Food: Monday-Friday: 12-9; Saturday: 12-8; Sunday: 12-6
& ❀ ➣ *but limited to certain times*
☎ *020 7223 3549*
Clapham Junction railway and buses 344, 319, 345, 49 and 44
Beers: Greene King IPA and Adnams are available regularly. Guest beers include Young's Special and Fuller's London Pride.

This large, handsome, three-storey mid-Victorian building also incorporates an acclaimed and well-established fringe theatre. Decorated with old programmes and theatrical bric-a-brac, there are comfortable sofas and chairs. There's a pub quiz held every Tuesday. Food includes Caesar salad, sausage and mash, baguettes and jacket potatoes.

...also worth trying

The Beehive

197 St Johns Hill (Clapham Junction railway)
An old-fashioned, cosy, local Fuller's pub in the heart of what is traditionally recognised as Young's brewery's home turf. Good, reasonably priced, home cooked meals are available at lunchtimes, Monday to Saturday.

Duke of Cambridge

228 Battersea Bridge Road (Clapham Junction railway)
A multi award-winning Young's Pub near to Battersea Park with an up market menu that features dishes like tempura battered cod, lemon and thyme scented chicken and mushroom and chestnut risotto.

The Falcon

2 St John's Hill, Clapham Junction (Clapham Junction railway)
Holding the Guinness Book of Records' accolade for having the longest continuous bar in Britain, Fuller's London Pride and Bass are regularly available.

The Woodman

60 Battersea High Street, Battersea (Clapham Junction railway)
The ales available in this cosy and comfortable local have travelled from Dorset to Battersea and include Badger Best, Champion and Tanglefoot. There's live music every fortnight and a pub quiz every Tuesday. Food includes steak and kidney suet pudding, blackened chicken and crispy bacon salad and pepper and mushroom pasta.

SW12

The Nightingale

97 Nightingale Road, Balham

Open: Monday-Saturday: 11-11; Sunday: 12-10.30
Food: Monday-Friday: 12-2.15 and 7-9.30; Sat and Sunday: 1-3
♿ ❀ ☃
☎ 020 8673 1637
Clapham South tube and Wandsworth Common railway
Beers: *Young's Bitter, Special and Triple A are available regularly. Seasonal ales also come from Young's brewery.*
A commitment to the community is reflected in the Nightingale's renowned local fundraising, which has netted more than £300, 000 since 1978 and features an annual Windsor to Putney walk along the Thames, organised by the regulars.
A traditional 150 year-old cosy Young's pub, with a large central bar, the pub has won various community 'pub of the year' awards. There's a monthly pub quiz and food includes Thai fish cakes, steak and kidney pudding, mushroom stroganoff and Stilton and pasta bake.

...also worth trying

The Grove

30 Oldridge Road, Balham (Clapham South tube)
Local CAMRA members say they cannot recommend the Grove 'highly enough'. Built in the 1870s, this large but cosy Young's pub retains its original gin palace style décor and serves a consistently first class pint.

SW13

The Bull's Head

373 Lonsdale Road, Barnes

Open: Monday-Saturday: 11-11; Sunday: 12-10.30
Food: Monday-Saturday: 12-11; Sunday: 12-3
👍 ❀ ⏃
☎ 020 8876 5241
Barnes Bridge railway station and bus 209
Beers: Young's Bitter, Special and Triple A. Guests are all from Young's brewery and include Winter Warmer.

Now celebrating its 40th anniversary of hosting live jazz and blues, there have been 16,350 concerts so far at the Bull's Head at Barnes.

Landlord Daniel Fleming believes the statistics constitute a record – of the non-vinyl type, of course. You can see a variety of musicians, many of whom are world famous, appearing in the room off the main bar every evening and twice on Sundays.

Overlooking the river, this large Victorian pub also boasts the longest unbroken view of the University boat race of any pub on the Thames.

Inside, the bright and airy main bar features bare floorboards, an ornate plasterwork ceiling, brass globe lighting and two open fireplaces. In addition to the lovingly tended Young's beers, the island bar dispenses around 80 different kinds of whisky and offers one of the largest wine lists in the capital, with a dozen kinds of champagne, 10 ports and 30 or so different wines available by the glass. For those not tempted by the fine array of alcohol, there's also an extensive coffee menu.

Food includes roast of the day, the pub's own recipe sausages, pies, casseroles, freshly made vegetable soup, vegetable bake and a selection of Thai food in the evening.

Coach and Horses

27 High Street, Barnes

Open: Mon-Thurs: 11-3 and 5.30-11; Friday-Saturday: 11-11; Sunday: 12-4 and 7-10.30
Food: Monday-Sunday: 12-2.30
❀ ⏃ only in the garden
☎ 020 8876 2695
Barnes Bridge railway station and bus 209
Beers: Young's Bitter, Special and Triple A. Guests are all from Young's brewery and include Winter Warmer.

This extremely popular old coaching inn really comes into its own in the summer, with its huge child-friendly garden and barbeques. For grown-ups, there's also a flood-lit boules pitch.

Inside the smallish main bar, there are padded bench seats, an open fireplace and an attractive etched bowed glass window. Hops around the bar, barrels incorporated into its design and more barrels used as stools and tables denote its devotion to high quality real ales. The pub was voted a CAMRA regional winner in 1998 and regularly appears in the *Good Beer Guide*.

Food includes hot toasted Italian paninis, spicy meat balls – served with what the pub's extrovert landlord describes as 'a mountain of mash' – chicken tikka masala and ravioli filled with mushrooms.

The Rose of Denmark

28 Cross Street, Barnes

Open: *Monday-Saturday: 11-11; Sunday: 12-10.30*
Food: *All day and every day*
& ❀
☎ *020 8392 1761*
Barnes Bridge railway station and buses 209, 418 and 33
Beers: *Brakspear Bitter, Woodforde's Wherry and Timothy Taylor's Landlord are all available regularly.*

A street corner local, the Rose of Denmark is a little off the Barnes beaten track of pubs, but worth seeking out, not least for the opportunity to sup a pint of Woodforde's Wherry – a fairly rare find in the capital's watering holes. Food at this comfortable and surprisingly roomy venue includes scampi or chicken and chips, garlic mushrooms and vegetable samosas and is served all day, every day.

The Sun

7 Church Road, Barnes

Open: *Monday-Saturday: 11-11; Sunday: 12-10.30*
Food: *Monday-Friday: 12-2.45 and 6-10; Saturday: 12-2.30 and 6-10; Sunday: 12-3.30*
& ❀ ℗
☎ *020 8876 5256*
Barnes or Barnes Bridge railway station and bus 209
Beers: *Tetley Bitter, Wadworth 6X, Adnams Bitter, Fuller's London Pride and Bass are available regularly.*

With its pretty as a picture location opposite Barnes Pond, the Sun is a well-known and popular local landmark. Bearing all the hallmarks of a countryside pub – friendly locals, good beer and even water bowls for the dogs – it's hard to believe you're still in the capital.

Aptly described by my drinking buddy as "a big, small pub", it features large areas adjoined by smaller, more intimate rooms. The room off to the right of the bar seems to be the most popular with the card-playing locals, while a no-smoking area at the rear continues the 'rustic country meets Victorian parlour' feel, complete with over-sized Welsh dresser. It's easy to get lost amidst the labyrinthine layout, so probably well worth telling your friends precisely where you'll be, if you arrange to meet them here.

There's live music on Tuesday evenings and food includes home made chilli, fish and chips, broccoli and cheese bake and a Thai menu from 6pm in the evening.

Ye White Hart

The Terrace, Barnes

Open: *Monday-Friday: 11-3 and 5.30-11; Saturday: 11-11; Sunday: 12-10.30*
Food: *Monday to Saturday: 12-2.30 and 6.30-10; Sunday: 12-2.30*
❀
☎ *020 8876 5777*
Barnes Bridge railway station and bus 209
Beers: *Young's Bitter, Special and Triple A.*

Floor length windows across the entire back wall of this grand Victorian pub, coupled with a riverside terrace, provide the perfect spot to cheer on your favoured oarsmen, as they approach the end of the University boat race course.

Given the oars above the bar, rowing is clearly a passion and I'm guessing that rugby is held in similarly high esteem, judging by the kilted but well-behaved gents surrounding the elliptical bar.

The pub features high ceilings and a drawing room style décor, complete with fresh flowers, while the soft terracotta colour scheme and open fire ensure Ye White Hart feels warm and cosy, even on a chill winter's evening. Food too is reminiscent of hotter climes, with a reasonably priced tapas menu, featuring such Spanish delicacies as merguez sausages, patatas bravas and garlic mushrooms. For those looking for more substantial alternatives, you can choose from options like wild boar sausages and mash, braised lamb shank and tortellini gorgonzola.

SW14

The Hare and Hounds

216 Upper Richmond Road West, East Sheen

Open: *Monday-Saturday: 11-11; Sunday: 12-10.30*
Food: *Monday-Saturday: 12-3 and 6-9; Sunday: 12-3*
❀ ☎
☎ *020 8876 4304*

Mortlake railway
Beers: *Young's Bitter, Special and Triple A are available regularly. Seasonal ales also come from Young's brewery.*

Budding Ronnie O'Sullivans take note: this pub boasts a full size snooker table in its rear saloon. Featuring a large, comfortable, oak paneled lounge, there's a children's play area in the walled garden. Food includes steak and kidney pie, scampi and sausage and mash.

SW15

Duke's Head

8 Lower Richmond Road

Open: *Monday-Saturday: 11-11; Sunday: 12-10.30*
Food: *Monday-Friday: 12-3 and 6-10; Saturday: 12-10; Sunday: 12-4*
&
☎ *020 8788 2552*
Putney Bridge tube
Beers: *Young's Bitter, Special and Triple A are available regularly. Seasonal ales also come from Young's brewery.*

The large bay windows looking out across the river give you the perfect vantage point to watch the start of the annual University boat race, which begins at a spot almost opposite the pub. Early Victorian, with ornate glasswork inside and out, comfy chairs, sofas and an open fire in winter, food includes steak and kidney pudding, bangers and mash and vegetarian lasagne.

The Green Man

Putney Heath, Putney

Open: *Monday-Saturday: 11-11; Sunday: 12-10.30*
Food: *Summer: 12-3 and 7-9 daily; winter: 12-2.30*
❀ ☛
☎ *020 8788 8096*
Putney/East Putney railway and buses 14, 85, 170, 93, and 39
Beers: *Young's Bitter, Special and Triple A are available regularly. Seasonal ales also come from Young's brewery.*

Sitting on the edge of Putney Heath, the pub dates back to around 1700 and was once the haunt of highwaymen. A two-bar pub, you can play traditional pub games, like shove ha'penny and ringing the bull. There's a quiz every Tuesday evening. Food includes Jamaican chicken curry, cottage pie, home cooked ham, mushroom ravioli and Boston bean casserole.

Halfmoon

93 Lower Richmond Road, Putney

Open: *Monday-Saturday: 11-11; Sunday: 12-10.30*
Food: *Fresh baguettes daily but no meals*
& ❀

☎ *020 8780 9383*

Putney Bridge tube
Beers: *Young's Bitter, Special and Triple A are available regularly. Seasonal ales also come from Young's brewery.*

It may only be rock and roll, but if you like it, then Putney's Halfmoon is the pub for you. The Rolling Stones are amongst the household names that have strutted their stuff here, swapping their Zimmer frames for guitars in May 2000, while U2 played their first London gig here back in the days when Bono's talent far outweighed the size of his ego – in other words, too many years ago to remember.

Music is live, seven nights a week in one of the oldest venues in the capital. On Sunday lunchtimes there is free jazz from 1pm until 4pm. The rest of the week may feature rock, blues, funk, jazz, pop or alternative. The beer is Young's and although there are no meals, there are fresh baguettes daily. Hell, who needs food when you're a rock legend?

SW16

Pied Bull

498 Streatham High Road, Streatham

Open: *Monday-Saturday: 11-11; Sunday: 12-10.30*
Food: *Monday-Saturday: 12-2.30 and 6.30-9.30; Sunday: 12-3*
& ❀ ☛ ⓟ

☎ *020 8764 4003*

Streatham/Norbury railway and buses 250, 159, 60 and 50
Beers: *Young's Bitter, Special and Triple A are available regularly. Seasonal ales also come from Young's brewery.*

With its listed frontage and friendly local following, the Pied Bull is widely acknowledged to be Streatham's best pub – not that there's a great deal of competition for the accolade. Close to Streatham Common, part of this large and comfortable local was once a coaching inn. Attractions include an open fire in winter and an absence of piped music. Instead, there's karaoke on Friday evening and live jazz on Sundays. Food includes homemade pies, traditional roasts and lasagne.

SW17

...also worth trying

Gorringe Park

29 London Road, Tooting (Tooting railway)
A two-bar Young's pub, with a cosy wood panelled lounge, just a few doors away from the railway station.

Prince of Wales

646 Garratt lane, Summerstown
This is a three-roomed down-to-earth, well-maintained local, with a handsome tiled exterior, serving Young's beers. It's handy for Wimbledon Greyhound Stadium and the Sunday Market.

SW18

The Cat's Back

86 Point Pleasant, Wandsworth

Open: Monday to Thursday: 12-3 and 5.30-11; Friday and Saturday: 11-11; Sunday: 12-10.30
Food: Monday-Friday: 12-3 and 7-10; Saturday: None; Sunday: 12-5

☎ *020 8877 0818*
East Putney or Wandsworth Town railway and buses 220 and 270
Beers: Eccleshall Slater's Bitter, O'Hanlons Blakeley's Best and Port Stout are available regularly. Occasional seasonal beers are available.

As a cat lover, I can quite appreciate that you might be overcome with emotion when your errant feline finally returns home safe and sound – but enough to christen your pub after the event? Well that's precisely what happened when the fretful licensees returned from their holidays, expecting bad news about their lost moggy, and instead found a friend had placed a large sign in the window saying 'The cat's back'.

A small one bar free house, there's been a pub on site since 1865, when it was called, rather more traditionally, Ye Old House at Home. Décor features an eccentric collection of artefacts – or junk, depending on your point-of-view. These include an assortment of accordions, a tree struck by lightening, lots of mirrors, family photographs, a ship's figurehead and work from local artists. There's a large stained glass window behind the bar and seating is a mish-mash of chairs, sofas, chaise longues and even the odd throne – presumably ear-marked for any stray cats in need of pampering.

The pub is on the Wandsworth heritage trail and is close to the Thames and Wandsworth Park. There are live bands on Sundays and food is a cut above average pub grub, with dishes changing daily. Options may include salmon steak with a dill sauce, Mediterranean vegetable pasta, beef bourguignon and a homemade soup. There's a traditional roast on Sundays. For Wandsworth dwellers, it's the cat's whiskers...

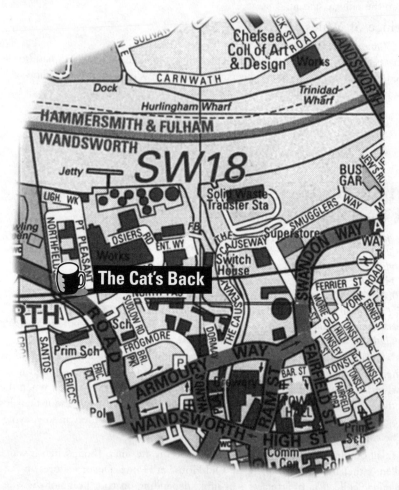

The Cat's Back

The Queen Adelaide

35 Putney Bridge Road, Wandsworth

Open: *Monday-Saturday: 11-11; Sunday: 12-10.30*
Food: *Monday-Saturday: 12-2.30 and 7-9.30; Sunday: 12-2.30*
❀ *Ch: Only in the garden*
☎ *020 8894 1695*
East Putney tube and Wandsworth Town railway
Beers: *Young's Bitter, Special and Triple A are available regularly. Seasonal ales also come from Young's brewery.*

Watch out for the seemingly nice bloke who has a winning way in persuading you to confess your worldly secrets – it might just be that Nasty Nick from television's Big Brother series, as he's a regular here. If it all gets too much, you can always escape to the attractive large garden of this traditional English pub that was rebuilt in 1838. There's a pub quiz and food available most lunchtimes and evenings – but the menu was about to change as we went to press.

The Spread Eagle

71 High Street, Wandsworth

Open: *Monday-Saturday: 11-11; Sunday: 12-10.30*
Food: *Monday-Friday: 12-2.30*
♿
☎ *020 8877 9809*
Wandsworth Town railway and buses 220 and 37
Beers: *Young's Bitter, Special and Triple A are available regularly. Seasonal ales also come from Young's brewery.*

Etched mirrors, two open fires, lots of original dark wood panels and Victorian entrances and archways onto the High Street enhance the old-fashioned, traditional feel of this Young's local. Originally a coaching inn dating back to the mid-1700s, it was rebuilt in 1898. Food makes the most of the Young's range of brews and includes steak and ale pie, made with Young's Special, and plaice in Young's Pilsner batter. There's also chilli con carne, vegetable samosa and vegetarian burgers.

...also worth trying

Grapes

39 Fairfield Street, Wandsworth (Wandsworth Town railway)
A small, traditional one-bar Young's local, with wood panelling and mirrors, dating from 1833. There's an award-winning garden and plans for a conservatory.

Old Sergeant

104 Garratt Lane, Wandsworth (Earlsfield railway)
About five minutes walk from Wandsworth town centre, this two-bar Young's pub
originally dates from the 18th century.

SW19

Hand in Hand

6 Crooked Billet, Wimbledon

Open: *Monday-Saturday: 11-11; Sunday: 12-10.30*
Food: *Monday-Saturday: 12-2.30 and 7-10; Sunday: 12-2.30 and 7-9*
&. ❀ ☙
☎ *020 8946 5720*

Wimbledon tube and railway; buses 200 and 93
Beers: *Young's Bitter, Special and Triple A are available regularly. Seasonal ales also
come from Young's brewery.*

Close to Wimbledon Common, this is a popular destination on balmy summer's
evenings, when the clientele tends to spill onto the small green outside, which
doubles as a garden extension. In the winter months, you'll have to make do with
a weekly pub quiz. Food includes the apparently world famous homemade 'Hand
burger', roasted vegetable lasagne, rib-eye steak, Mediterranean risotto and vegetable chilli and rice.

The Rose and Crown

55 High Street, Wimbledon Village

Open: *Monday-Saturday: 11-11; Sunday: 12-10.30*
Food: *Monday-Friday: 12-2.30 and 6-9; Saturday: 12-3 and 6-9; Sunday: 12-3*
&. ❀ ☙ *in certain areas;* ℗
☎ *020 8947 4713*

Wimbledon tube and railway and bus 93
Beers: *Young's Bitter, Special and Triple A are available regularly. Seasonal ales also
come from Young's brewery.*

You know you're in safe hands in the Rose and Crown, as the landlord, Richard
Williamson, was a regional winner of the Innkeeper of the Year Award 2000. A
traditional Victorian high street pub, with a conservatory, there's an open fire in
winter and an attractive courtyard garden in the summer, when the pub hosts
occasional opera nights. Food includes giant Yorkshire pudding filled with
Cumberland sausage and mash, steak and kidney pie, vegetable pancake and tagliatelle with a creamy mushroom sauce. Plans are afoot to add a 12-bedroom hotel,
but the licensee promises that the village pub atmosphere remains sacrosanct.

The Sultan

78 Norman Road

Open: Monday-Saturday: 12-11; Sunday: 12-10.30
Food: None
& ❀ ☎ *only in the garden;* ℗
☎ *020 8542 4532*
Colliers Wood and South Wimbledon tube; buses 57, 200 and 156
Beers: Hop Back Summer Lightning, GFB, Entire Stout, Thunderstorm and Crop Circle
*are available regularly. Seasonal ales also come from the Hop Back brewery and change
monthly.*

For devotees of Wiltshire's Hop Back brewery, the Sultan is a place of pilgrimage.
Although it may not score too highly on the looks front, the award–winning
brews in this traditional ale house more than make up for a lack of glamour.
Originally bombed in the war and rebuilt in the 1950s, the pub was CAMRA's
local pub of the year in 2000. There's a quiz every Tuesday evening, a barbeque
during the summer months at weekends and a beer festival held every September,
with 20 guest beers. Especially popular amongst real ale fans is the beer club, held
every Wednesday evening between 6 and 9pm, when all real ales are £1.50 a pint.
Book your bar stool now...

...also worth trying

Brewery Tap

68 High Street, Wimbledon (Wimbledon tube/railway)
In the centre of Wimbledon Village, this small, friendly pub is well supported by
local CAMRA members, as it offers a wide range of guest beers, featuring smaller
and more remote breweries. Recently refurbished, the locals love its excellent bar
food and snacks, with the marinated olives and anchovies a particular highlight.

CARSHALTON

Windsor Castle

378 Carshalton Road, Carshalton

Open: Monday-Saturday: 11-11; Sunday: 12-10.30
Food: Monday-Saturday: 12-2 and 7-9.30; Sunday: 12-4
& ❀ Ch: Only before 6pm; ℗
☎ *020 8669 1191*
Carshalton Beeches
Beers: Bass, Fuller's London Pride, Wadworth 6X, Marston's Pedigree, Hancock's HB,

Greene King Abbot Ale, Shepherd Neame Spitfire and Young's Special are available regularly while a changing list of guests features Cottage, Arundel, O'Hanlons, Gale's and many micro-breweries.

This is a pub that takes the quality and choice of the beers it offers very seriously indeed – and their reward is to be voted local CAMRA pub of the year five years running. A single bar pub with a restaurant at one end, so far it has served more than 1, 700 guest ales. There's live music every Saturday night and food is more adventurous than most, featuring pan fried duck breast with a brandy and cream sauce, a selection of steaks cut to order, leek and gruyere crown, mushroom stroganoff and baked avocado.

...also worth trying

Greyhound

2 High Street, Carshalton (Carshalton railway)
Grade II listed, the Greyhound is back in business after a refit and a hotel extension at the back. The pub overlooks Carshalton ponds and boasts an atmospheric, unspoilt bar and well-kept beer.

Railway Tavern

47 North Street, Carshalton (Carshalton railway)
This friendly, traditional street corner local, close to the railway station and Carshalton Ponds, offers occasional live music. Decorated with railway memorabilia, the landlord is a Fuller's Master Cellarman. Food is basic and includes egg, ham or sausage with chips.

CHEAM

Claret Wine Bar

33 The Broadway, Cheam

Open: *Monday-Saturday: 11.30-11; Sunday: 12-10.30*
Food: *Monday-Saturday: 11.30-6; Sunday: 12-5*
&
☎ *020 8715 9002*
Cheam railway and buses 213, 154 and 726
Beers: *Shepherd Neame Masterbrew and Spitfire or Morland's Old Speckled Hen are available regularly and there are two guest beers that change every month.*

Set in the main shopping street, this smart bar is a blend of old and new. An oak frontage, light wood panelling and scrubbed wooden floors are joined by air conditioning and an à la carte restaurant upstairs that can be hired for private parties.

There's a weekly quiz night with free bar snacks, while other food includes sausage and mash, scampi, tortellini with spinach and carbonara with Mediterranean vegetables. There's also a curry night every Thursday.

...also worth trying

Prince of Wales

28 Malden Road (Cheam railway)
A smartly turned out, spacious local on the northern side of Cheam with a choice of well-kept ales.

KINGSTON-UPON-THAMES

The Bishop-Out-Of-Residence

2 Riverside Walk

Open: *Monday-Saturday: 11-11; Sunday: 12-10.30*
Food: *Monday-Saturday: 11.9.30; Sunday: 12-9*
❀ ☞
☎ *020 8546 4965*
Kingston-upon-Thames railway and all buses to Kingston
Beers: *Young's Bitter, Special and Triple A are available regularly. Guest and seasonal beers also come from Young's brewery.*

Looking out across the river to the grounds of Hampton Court Palace and Kingston Bridge, the pub's a modern building with a preservation order to retain its waterfront heritage. Food is freshly made every day and includes steak and kidney or steak and mushroom pie, chilli con carne, lasagne, vegetable pasta bake and quiche. On Sundays there's a choice of four traditional roasts with the usual trimmings.

Boaters

Canbury Gardens, Lower Ham Road

Open: *Monday-Saturday: 11-11 summer only – in winter the pub closes between 3-5.30pm; Sunday: 12-10.30*
Food: *Monday-Saturday: 12-2.30 and 7-9.30; Sunday: 12-2.30*
❀ ☞
☎ *020 8541 4672*
Kingston-upon-Thames railway, Richmond tube and bus 65
Beers: *Brakspear's and Greene King IPA are always available. There are usually three other guest ales that might include Young's, Gale's, Hancock's, Courage and Wadworth plus smaller breweries.*

With its prime riverside location and seating outside for hundreds, the Boaters is an ideal destination on a balmy summer's day – and should you choose to arrive in style by boat, you'll find exclusive mooring for pub customers here.

A two-week long annual beer festival – held every March and offering around 80 real ales on tap – is an added out of season attraction while other year-round entertainment includes a well-established live jazz session every Sunday evening, which has been successfully running for more than a decade. A more recent addition is a blues evening on Tuesday. Food includes steak and ale pie, shank of lamb, fillet steak, roasted vegetable lasagne and broccoli and cheese bake.

...also worth trying

Wych Elm

93 Elm Road (Kingston-upon-Thames railway)
One of only two Fuller's pubs in Kingston, the Wych Elm has retained both its bars. Entertainment includes occasional summer barbeques and live jazz. Food includes lamb chops, home made steak and kidney pie, liver and bacon and leek and Gruyere crown.

RICHMOND

The Marlborough

46 Friars Stile Road

Open: *Monday-Saturday: 12-11; Sunday: 12-10.30*
Food: *Monday-Fridayri: 12-3; Saturday: 12-6; Sunday: 12-9*
  ⅄ ✿ ⅃ *until 9pm*
☎ *020 8940 0572*
Richmond tube and bus 371
Beers: *Bass and Fuller's London Pride are available regularly.*

Just a two-minute stroll from Richmond Park, this long and narrow pub attracts a variety of well-known customers, including Jennifer Saunders and Mick Jagger. Perhaps they're enticed by the potential to secrete themselves away in its dark corners – although it would be hard to hide other visitors, like the England rugby team for instance, in one of them for long.

Those who seek a taste of notoriety for themselves, may like to participate in the pub's monthly 'culture-jam' sessions, where if you can sing, play an instrument or do something weird, wonderful and entertaining you're more than welcome to join in.

Outside is an acclaimed and extensive walled garden, where barbeques are held occasionally in the summer months. Other food includes rump steak, Caribbean chicken, vegetable and cheese bake and vegetable Kiev.

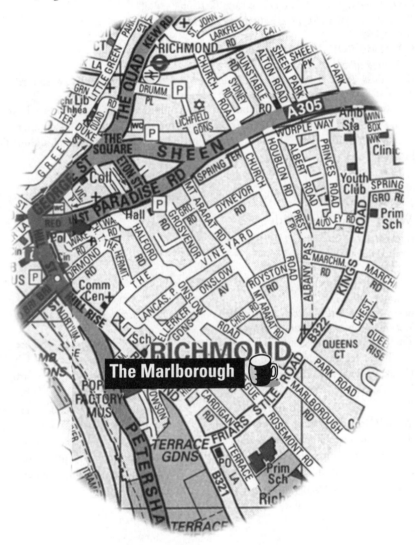

Triple Crown

15 Kew Foot Road

Open: Monday-Saturday: 11-11; Sunday: 12-10.30
Food: Monday-Fridayri: 12-2; Saturday: 12-3; Sunday: None
& ❀ ❧ ℗
☎ 020 8940 3805
Richmond tube
Beers: Bass, Timothy Taylor's Landlord and Shepherd Neame Spitfire may be featured amongst the pub's regularly changing four real ales.

The only true free house in Richmond, the Triple Crown is a thriving back street local with a loyal clientele. Small, friendly and relaxed, there's a long-standing quiz night on Tuesdays. Homemade food includes steak and ale pie, ploughman's lunch and vegetarian pasta.

White Cross

Water Lane, Riverside

Open: Monday-Saturday: 11-11; Sunday: 12-10.30
Food: Monday-Sunday: 12-3.30
❀ ❧
☎ 020 8940 6844
Richmond tube
Beers: Young's Bitter, Special and Triple A are available regularly. Guest and seasonal beers also come from Young's brewery.

The most famous riverside pub in Richmond, Gardeners' World fans who are puzzling over the unusual tree in the front patio may like to know that it's a Greek Whitebeam – reputedly the only one in Britain other than in the nearby Kew Gardens.

With its open fires, beautiful views of the Thames and well-kept Young's ales, the White Cross is a classic, but unfortunately you're unlikely to be the first to recognise its considerable charms, as it gets packed out with punters, particularly during the summer months. River level permitting, the riverside terrace is open during the summer and on sunny winter weekends. Food includes speciality sausages, nut roast and vegetable lasagne.

White Swan

26 Old Palace Lane

Open: Monday-Saturday: 11-11; Sunday: 12-10.30
Food: Monday-Friday: 12-3 and 7 until closing; Saturday: 12-4 and 7 until closing; Sunday: 12-4
  ぐ ❀ ☎
☎ *020 8940 0959*
Richmond tube
Beers: Fuller's London Pride, Courage Best and Directors and Brakspear's are available regularly. Guest ales might include Adnams or Marston's Pedigree.

Ducks in the extensive garden, a low-beamed ceiling and an à la carte menu, offering a traditional roast on Sundays, are some of the attractions of this 18th century country-style pub, which is hidden away in a picturesque street of cottages. Attracting a local clientele as well as the odd intrepid tourist, there's live music twice a month on Sunday evenings and a quiz held every Monday. A relatively new manager has boosted the choice of real ales available.

SURBITON

The Lamb Inn

73 Brighton Road

Open: Monday-Saturday: 11-11; Sunday: 12-10.30
Food: Monday-Saturday: 12-3; Sunday: 1-3
  ぐ ❀ ☎
☎ *020 8390 9229*
Surbiton railway
Beers: Greene King IPA, Young's Special and Marston's Pedigree are available regularly. Guest beers might include Badger's Tanglefoot, Black Sheep Special, Everards Tiger and Bateman's.

This small, one-bar local, with its wooden floors and black beams, offers a changing range of well-kept guest ales, in addition to three regular beers. In the summer there are occasional barbeques in the pleasant garden while other entertainment includes a quiz night every Tuesday and Karaoke on the first Saturday of every month. Food is standard pub fare of burgers, sausages, all day breakfast and ploughman's but includes a daily home-cooked special.

...also worth trying

Sutton

The Little Windsor
13 Greyhound Road (Sutton railway)
A small back-street local offering the full range of Fuller's ales and a freshly cooked daily special at lunchtime.

WALLINGTON

Duke's Head Hotel

6 Manor Road (Wallington railway)

This traditional award-winning Young's pub and hotel is in an attractive setting on the edge of Wallington Green.

WEST LONDON

W1

The Audley

41-43 Mount Street

Open: *Monday-Saturday: 11-11; Sunday: 12-10.30*
Food: *Monday-Saturday: 11-9.30; Sunday: 12-9*
♿ ✿ ☻
☎ *020 7499 1843*
Bond Street, Marble Arch or Green Park tube plus buses that run down Oxford Street
Beers: *Courage Best, Directors and Green King IPA all available regularly.*

Is this James Bond's local? Set in the heart of Mayfair, the Audley could be a prime choice for his usual 'shaken not stirred', not least as over the road is The Spy Shop, selling enough electronic surveillance equipment to reheat the Cold War. Meanwhile three doors down is the Counter Spy Shop, offering a range of bullet proof vests and other paraphernalia that I had previously thought only existed in particularly vivid imaginations or Boys Own comics.

Finding a seat in this busy, decidedly up-market pub almost proved to be mission impossible. With its handsome red brick and pink terracotta exterior, polished dark wood, large windows, red and gold plasterwork ceilings, original ornate glass chandeliers and two fine clocks in the bar, it's easy to see why the first Duke of Westminster insisted on a name change from the Bricklayer's Arms when he rebuilt it. Indeed he rejected the first set of plans submitted to him on the grounds that they were "too gin palacey".

There's no music, pool table or darts but there is a jazz night on Mondays. Food options include fish and chips, three cheese pasta, roast of the day, various salads and sandwiches – but as you might expect from the area, it's all a bit on the pricey side.

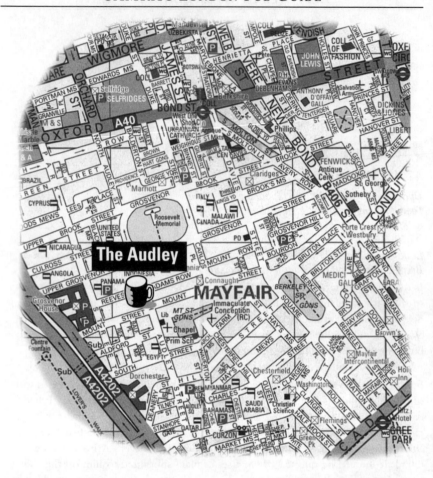

The Beehive

7 Homer Street

Open: *Monday to Thursday: 11-3 and 5.30-11; Friday and Saturday: 11-11; Sunday: 12-10.30*
Food: *Monday-Friday: 12-2.30*
&*but limited;* ❀
☎ *020 7262 6581*
Edgware Road tube plus buses 18 and 27
Beers: *Fuller's London Pride and Young's Bitter*

The Beehive is a real locals' local. That some of those locals should appear regularly on our television screens is really neither here nor there. But I must confess that, as an occasional reader of celebrity gossip magazines, spotting actress Wendy Richard – aka as Pauline Fowler, the downtrodden mistress of the launderette in

Eastenders – made my Saturday afternoon.

Tiny, with barely 30 seats, we couldn't avoid seeing the champagne cork pop to greet the arrival of Ms Richard. However, the fantasy of being in the presence of a star dimmed slightly when we saw she drank her favourite Moet from a sherry schooner – but at least she left the infamous cardigan at home.

Star spotting aside, the Beehive has attractive etched windows, a small fireplace and sepia tinted photographs of the local area. It also boasts the most eclectic collection of items above the bar, including Chinese style vases, a coffee grinder, models of horses and jockeys and two plastic pigeons. In a nutshell, the beer's well-kept, the banter is lively and the Beehive has true star quality.

The Coach and Horses

5 Bruton Street

Open: *Monday-Friday: 11-11; Saturday: 11-8; Sunday: closed*
Food: *Monday-Friday: 11-11; Sat 11-6*
& ☛
☎ *020 7629 4123*
Green Park and Oxford Circus tube
Beers: *Courage Best and Directors. Guest ale is usually Morland's Old Speckled Hen or Marston's Pedigree.*

Despite the fact that it's tiny, you really can't miss the Coach and Horses. At the risk of sounding like Prince Charles, it's a small, Tudor looking building, with heavy leaded windows, surrounded by six-storey concrete square boxes.

Just around the corner from Sothebys, this dimly lit and dark wood paneled, cosy pub seats probably no more than 25 people in the ground floor bar, ensuring that it's very friendly. We got chatting to a chap who had just bought an engagement ring that day from Tiffany's and clearly needed a stiff drink. We discovered he'd once lived four doors away from me in Haringey and the ring had cost more than his parents had paid for the house. Another round and we'd have been special guests at the wedding – it's that kind of pub.

For the peckish, food includes sausage and mash, fish or scampi and chips, five bean chilli and roasted pepper lasagne.

Coach and Horses

29 Greek Street

Open: *Monday-Saturday: 11-11; Sunday: 12-10.30*
Food: *Monday-Saturday: 12-11; Sunday: None*
& *but limited access to toilets*
☎ *020 7437 5920*
Tottenham Court Road, Piccadilly and Leicester Square tube

Beers: *Burton Ale, Fuller's London Pride and Pedigree are all available regularly*

No visitor to Soho can claim their trip is complete without spending at least an hour or two in the Coach and Horses.

Norman is the quintessential abrasive publican, lording it over a bizarre and diverse bunch of locals, voyeurs, wannabes and has-beens for more than 20 years. Sadly, the most famous of them all, famed columnist and celebrated inebriate, Jeffrey Bernard, has gone to prop up that great bar in the sky.

The décor is based around formica, food is sandwiches, all priced at a quid, there's no piped music or a jukebox, but there's nightly entertainment provided by the cast of regulars. It's the stuff of legends.

The Dog and Duck

18 Bateman Street

Open: *Monday-Friday: 12-11; Saturday: 5-11; Sunday: 6-10.30*
Food: *None – there's no kitchen*
☻, *during the day but no baby changing facilities*
☎ *020 7494 0697*
Tottenham Court Road tube
Beers: *Fuller's London Pride, Timothy Taylor's Landlord, Adnams Broadside and Tetley are available regularly. Seasonal ales might include Everards Tiger, Old Hookey, Charles Wells Bombardier, Shepherd Neame's Spitfire and others.*

Barely a 100 yards from Ronnie Scott's legendary jazz club, the small but perfectly formed Dog and Duck is a million miles away from all those loud, neon lit, fashionable but otherwise featureless bars found everywhere in Soho these days.

This is the area's oldest pub, and apparently Mozart "lived, played and composed" in 1764 for a year at a house just over the road. Its listed interior features beautiful Edwardian tiles in shades of green, gold and aquamarine, etched mirrors, a bevelled glass canopy over the top of the bar and a fireplace towards the pub's rear.

There's no food, fruit machines, pool tables or television – it's too tiny to waste valuable space on such fripperies – but there's interesting conversation, friendly bar staff and a wide and changing range of lovingly cared for beers.

A real find for despairing real ale drinkers in Soho, who've had their fill of plastic pubs – the only downside is that you're likely to be beating a well-trodden path to its welcoming door, ensuring it's almost always packed to its elegant rafters.

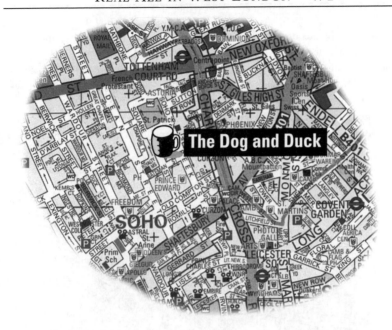

The Dover Castle

43 Weymouth Mews

Open: *Monday-Friday: 11.30-11; Saturday: 12-11; Sunday: closed*
Food: *Monday to Friday: 12-2.30 and 6-9; Saturday: 12-2.30*
☎ *020 7580 4412*
Regents Park, Great Portland Street or Oxford Circus
Beers: *Samuel Smith Old Brewery Bitter*

Tucked away in a tiny mews behind Harley Street and barely five minutes walk from Oxford Street and Regents Park, the Dover Castle is the kind of secret you should only share with those people you really like – as chances are, they're unlikely to stumble upon its existence any other way.

A genuine old English pub, records show that there have been licensed premises on this site since the 1770s. The décor is probably best described as shabby chic. There's a bar facing the front entrance and the largest of the pub's rooms is off to the right, with a small fireplace, wooden settles, wood panelling and prints of various sportsmen. Further down on the right, there's another completely partitioned room and, at the rear, a conservatory with a brightly painted, cheery looking mural-cum-collage of people standing at a bar, running across the entire length of one wall.

The bar staff are friendly and efficient and the cask conditioned Sam Smith's beer well looked after. We arrived just as they were changing the barrel and the obliging barman brought our drinks over to our table. It made a welcome change, as we'd just tried to visit another stunningly attractive Sam Smith's pub, The Champion in Wells Street, only to discover it did no real ale, the barman informing us that: "There's no call for it in central London. You'll be lucky to find anywhere that does it." Clearly fortune favours the brave.

Food includes Cumberland sausage and mash, cod fillet in beer batter with chips, home made pies, vegetable Kiev and chips and cannelloni, filled with spinach and ricotta.

Once the regular haunt of The Who in the days when their recording studios were opposite, we had to leave a little faster than I would have liked as the Greater Bellied One insisted on singing along to the Pink Floyd album they were playing, presumably hoping to be discovered by a rock and roll talent scout. Needless to say we're still waiting for the phone call…

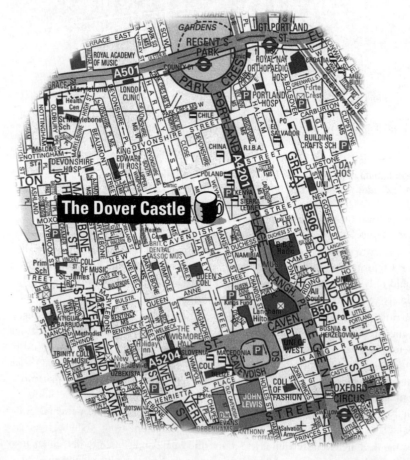

The George

1 D'Arblay Street

Open: Monday-Friday: 11-11; Saturday: 12-11; Sunday: 3-10.30
Food: Monday to Friday: 11-3 and Saturday: 12-3
☎ *020 7439 1911*
Oxford Circus or Tottenham Court Road tube
Beers: Tetley and Wadworth 6X.

The George and I didn't get off to the best of starts, as when I asked for a pint of Tetley, the barmaid attempted to give me the hideous "smoothflow" version. It was hard to recover from the hiccup.

Although it looks like a traditional Soho corner pub, with wooden floors, large windows and an ornate plasterwork ceiling, on a Saturday night it was just too brash and smoky to appease my 40 something sensibilities. Attracting mainly those who work in the music industry, a decade or two ago I expect I'd have loved it. Food is a selection of toasties.

The George

55 Great Portland Street

Open: Monday-Friday: 11-11; Saturday: 11-6; Sunday: 7-10.30
Food: Monday to Friday: 11-3 and 5-9; Saturday: 11-4; Sunday: none
☎ *020 7636 0863*
Oxford Circus tube and buses that run along Oxford Street or Regent Street
Beers: Greene King IPA and Abbot Ale, Fuller's London Pride, Morland's Old Speckled Hen and Marston's Pedigree are available regularly. Guest beers include Ruddles County, Theakston's Old Peculiar, Everards Tiger and others.

The famous conductor and founder of the Proms, Sir Henry Wood, christened the pub 'the Gluepot' in 1930. He used to rehearse the BBC Symphony Orchestra in the Queen's Hall, between the pub and Broadcasting House. During breaks, his musicians would venture to the George and were so often found enjoying the bar's delights, rather than practising on their instruments, that he joked their bottoms became stuck to the pub's seats. The entrance leading off Mortimer Street commemorates the tale.

Just around the corner from BBC radio headquarters, today it's an ideal venue for BBC Radio 4 groupies, as the crowd from the Loose Ends show, including Ned Sherrin and Arthur Smith, decamp here at lunchtime on Saturdays. Other associated luminaries include Dylan Thomas, who wrote here, and George Orwell, who mentions the pub in his novel, 1984.

An elegant Victorian pub, there's dark wood panelling throughout, which is dotted with original hunting scene ceramics that date from around 1890. The authentic mirrors have been acid etched and inlaid with gilt and there's an array of brass and copper – note the plaque depicting 'Service at the George'.

Food includes fish and chips, steak and kidney pie, vegetable pancakes, salmon and tarragon fishcakes and vegetable masala and rice.

The Golden Eagle

59 Marylebone Lane

Open: *Monday-Saturday: 11-11; Sunday: 12-10.30*
Food: *Monday to Friday: 12-2.45*
☎ *020 7935 3228*
Bond Street tube
Beers: Brakspear's, Fuller's London Pride and Adnams are available regularly. Guest beers include beers from Adnams, Thwaites and Timothy Taylor.

Just off the busy Marylebone High Street and on the corner of Bulstrode Street, this small, attractive free house hosts live piano and sing-a-long nights on Thursday and Friday evenings, making a welcome change from the ubiquitous karaoke.

Newly repainted in gentle pastel colours of yellow and grey, with a blue carpet, the etched glass behind the bar features a Golden Eagle, a pleasant reminder of where you are, just in case you drink too much of their well-kept ale and forget. Food includes Biggles home made sausages, sandwiches and ploughman's lunches.

The Pillars of Hercules

7 Greek Street

Open: *Monday-Saturday: 11-11; Sunday: 12-10.30*
Food: *Monday to Saturday: All day and Sunday: 12-6*

&

☎ 020 7437 1179

Oxford Circus, Tottenham Court Road, Leicester Square and Piccadilly tube
Beers: Marston's Pedigree, Courage Directors and Theakston's Best Bitter are available regularly. Guest ales might include beers from Thwaites, Skinners, Shepherd Neame, Smiles, Everards and Bateman's breweries.

Although a pub has stood on this site for more than 300 years, there's nothing dated about the crowd who manage to squeeze themselves into this busy Soho venue, spilling out onto the pavement in summer.

There's a real emphasis on cask-conditioned ale in this small, traditional looking pub, with a changing list of approximately 25 guest ales a month – so who says youth culture and real ale don't mix? Food includes all-in-one pies, filled Yorkshire puddings, salmon pasta melt and mushroom pepper pot.

The Ship

134 New Cavendish Street

Open: Monday-Saturday: 11-11 closed Saturday and Sunday
Food: Monday to Friday – toasted sandwiches only
❀
☎ 020 7636 6301
Great Portland Street tube
Beers: Bass

Rebuilt in 1887, the Ship is a traditional, cosy free house, ringed with benches on the pavement outside and some rather fine looking large bay trees in tubs. Look up and there's the BT Tower in all its glory. Inside, it's crammed with brass, Wenlock and Bass brewery fittings and naval artifacts. Food is a selection of toasted sandwiches. Note it's closed at the weekend.

The Spice of Life

37-39 Romilly Street, Cambridge Circus

Open: Monday-Saturday: 11-11; Sunday: 12-10.30
Food: Monday to Friday: 12-10; Saturday: 12-8; Sunday: 12-7
Disabled toilets are being added, so it's worth checking with the pub; ❀
☎ 020 7437 7013
Leicester Square tube and numerous buses
Beers: McMullen's Country, AK and Gladstone are available regularly. Guest beers also come from McMullen's and might include Winters Tale and Royal Cheer.

A Soho landmark with its velvet drapes, plush upholstery and dark wood panelling, it's hard to imagine that back in the 1970s, the Sex Pistols drank here.

Its castle-like listed exterior, complete with two turrets at the top, and its prime position, facing Cambridge Circus, always inspires me to think of it as the gatekeeper to Bohemia. Beyond its boundaries you suddenly find yourself in the network of Soho streets where anything could happen – all that's certain is you will spend more money than you can afford and have a monster-sized hangover to show for it. But perhaps that's just me. The Spice is also next door to 'Les Mis' and just a few minutes walk from Chinatown, Oxford Circus and Covent Garden.

Entertainment includes live jazz on Monday and Wednesday evenings and comedy nights coming soon – check with the pub for more details. Food includes lamb shank, a Mediterranean platter with olives, tzatziki and feta cheese, veggie sausages and mash and nachos with guacamole.

The Red Lion

1 Waverton Street

Open: Monday-Friday: 11.30-11; Saturday: 6-11; Sunday: 12-3 and 6-10.30
Food: Monday to Friday: 12-3; Saturday: 6-9.30; Sunday: 12-2.30 and 6-9.30

☎ *020 7499 1307*
Green Park tube
Beers: Greene King IPA, Courage Best and Directors and Theakston's Best are available regularly. Greene King Abbot Ale is sometimes a guest beer.

Sitting in the Red Lion, it's hard to believe that you're in the heart of Mayfair in the capital city, rather than some idyllic country village miles from traffic congested streets.

Covered in ivy – to the extent that looking up at the pub from Charles Street, all you can see of its name is "ion" – apparently this is singer Tom Jones' favourite watering hole when he's in town. Nearby, there's a plethora of blue plaques, including the homes of writer Somerset Maugham, from 1911 until 1919, that dedicated follower of fashion, Beau Brummel, until 1840, and even King William IV was a neighbour for a year in 1826, before he acceded to the throne in 1830. The pub has wooden floors, wood panelling and stained glass above the bar, while wooden settles and benches provide the seating. There are no machines or music but good food is offered at lunchtimes and evenings, both in the bar and at the à la carte restaurant. In the pub, food options might include Cumberland sausage and mash, Cajun chicken sandwich, fish and chips or stuffed aubergines.

The Woodstock

11 Woodstock Street

Open: *Monday-Saturday: 11-11; Sunday: 12-10.30*
Food: *Monday to Saturday: 11-11 and Sunday: 12-10*
⚜ ☎ *during the day*
☎ *020 7408 2008*
Bond Street tube
Beers: Theakston's Best and Old Peculiar, Courage Directors, and Greene King Abbot Ale are all available regularly. Guests might include Shepherd Neame's Spitfire or Early Bird or beers from the Bateman's range.

Just off Oxford Street, almost opposite Debenhams department store, the Woodstock provides a handy refuge for those who've shopped until they've dropped. It's cosy, warm and friendly, the clientele a mix of weary shoppers, nearby office workers and regulars.

Inside this small pub there's lots of dark Victorian paneling and a fireplace and outside there's a few benches that give a good vantage point in summer to watch the crowds go by. On tap, are three or four well-kept real ales, usually including an interesting guest beer. Food includes the pub's special all in one pies, beef and Yorkshire pudding, beer battered fish and chips and homemade leek and potato broth.

Ye Grapes

16 Shepherd Market, Mayfair

Open: *Monday-Friday: 11-11; Saturday: 12-11; Sunday: 12-3 and 6-10.30*
Food: *Monday to Friday: 12.30-2*
Green Park tube
Beers: Boddingtons, Fuller's London Pride, Timothy Taylor's Landlord, Marston's Pedigree, Flowers IPA and Wadworth's 6X.

Set amidst the lovely area of Shepherd Market – with its decidedly posh dellies, a few specialist shops and restaurants – Ye Grapes is a traditional Victorian pub, dating from 1882, where the clientele is a happy mix of regulars, some students and a few tourists.

An L-shaped room, it features mostly dark wooden floorboards with two raised and carpeted seating areas, one at the front and another at the rear. The green wallpapered walls are dotted with a strange mix of risqué prints of 1920s ladies, daring to bare their suspenders, and large numbers of stuffed birds and fish. For those who prefer to eat the fruits of the sea, rather than preserve them for posterity, there's a fresh fish shop around the corner where the intrepid cook can buy a live lobster.

Helpful staff offer tasters of any beer that you fancy trying before committing yourself to buy a pint. Food includes fish and chips, of course, and the usual pasta, sandwiches and ploughman's lunches.

...also worth trying

Barley Mow

8 Dorset Street (Baker Street tube)
Owned by Nicholsons and a listed heritage inn, this interesting pub features two small completely enclosed wooden cubicles once used to enable a long-gone publican to conduct his pawn-broking business over the bar. With the price of a pint reaching sky-high proportions, it's a lucrative sideline that might just come back into fashion. Real ales might include Adnams, Tetley's or Greene King IPA.

The Guinea

30 Bruton Place (Bond Street or Green Park tube)
In a quiet mews near to Berkley Square, this Young's pub is perhaps more famous for its attached small restaurant, which has the long-standing reputation for offering some of the best steaks in town.

The Three Greyhounds

25 Greek Street (Leicester Square tube)
Once my favourite pub in Soho, you could rely on finding a friendly mixed crowd, good conversation and a well-kept pint of Adnams. Now the jury's out, as it decided to change tempo, replacing its gentle ambience with brash, ear-splitting music. Fingers, toes and eyes crossed that by the time you read this, it will have seen the error of its ways and resumed normal service.

W2

The Archery Tavern

4 Bathurst Street, Paddington

Open: Monday-Saturday: 11-11; Sunday: 12-10.30
Food: Monday-Sunday: 12-3 and 6-9.30
 ♿ ❉ ✓
☏ *020 7402 4916*
Lancaster Gate tube
Beers: Badger Best, Champion Ale, Tanglefoot and Sussex Ale are all available regularly.

The clip clop of horses' hooves may be an unusual sound in the city, but it's a regular event at the Archery Tavern, as the pub is next door to Hyde Park riding stables.

Set in a quiet cul-de-sac close to Lancaster Gate and originally dating from the mid-1800s, the pub was built on the site of the archery ground owned by the Royal Toxopholite Society. A useful word for Call My Bluff enthusiasts, a toxopholite literally means 'lover of the bow'.

Essentially the Tavern comprises three rooms, fittingly separated by archways, with a central bar, wood panelling and a high ceiling. A large stained glass depiction of an archer divides the main area from the back room, where there are bare floorboards and piped music – the rest of the pub is jukebox free.

Those in need of entertainment can choose from the selection of board games on offer or take part in the Sunday evening quiz. Food includes steak and kidney pudding, chicken, leek and Stilton pie, mushroom stroganoff and vegetarian fajhita wraps.

Bridge House

13 Westbourne Terrace Road, Little Venice

Open: Monday-Saturday: 12-11; Sunday: 12-10.30
Food: Monday-Saturday: 12-3 and 6-9.30; Sunday: 12-3 and 6-9
 & ✿
☎ 020 7432 1361
Warwick Avenue and Paddington tube; buses 6 and 18
Beers: Fuller's London Pride and Bass are available regularly.

A well-established upstairs theatre, serving up comedy shows and fringe productions every day of the week, is one of the attractions of this canal-side pub, which neighbours Little Venice. Food includes fish, steak, Sunday roast, roasted vegetable lasagne, spicy bean burgers and jacket potatoes.

Fountains Abbey

109 Praed Street, Paddington

Open: Monday-Saturday: 11-11; Sunday: 12-10.30
Food: Monday-Saturday: All day, every day
 & ✿ ☎, *until 6pm*
☎ 020 7723 2364
Paddington tube and rail
Beers: Courage Best and Directors, Theakstons Best, Morland's Old Speckled Hen and Charles Wells Bombardier are available regularly. Guest ales include Gale's HSB,

Marston's Pedigree, Badger's Tanglefoot, Exmoor Gold and Shepherd Neame's Bishop's Finger.

Legend has it that mould spores from the Fountains Abbey flew through Sir Alexander Fleming's laboratory window, on the second storey of St Mary's Hospital overlooking the pub, leading him to the discovery of penicillin in 1928. If you want to test the veracity of this claim, visit the laboratory museum opposite the pub.

Built in 1824, there is an original – in all senses of the word – listed fireplace in the main room, some wood panelling, a few glass screens and a raised seating area on the left. Most of the floor is bare, with a carpeted area on the right and there are a few too many chalkboards for my liking. Noisy and busy, even on Friday afternoon, it's difficult to imagine Sir Alexander unwinding over a quiet pint after a hard day at the microscope, but apparently he was a regular here.

Food includes fish and chips, all in one pies with beef, chicken or lamb, sandwiches, burgers, mushroom pepper pot and red pepper lasagne. There's a function room upstairs, available for private hire.

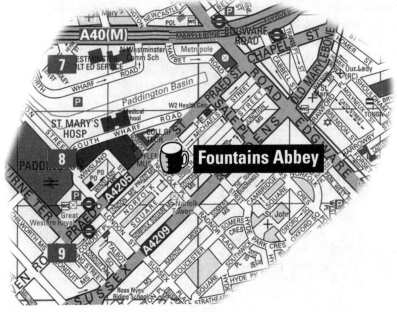

The Mad Bishop and Bear

First Floor, The Lawn, Paddington Station

Open: *Monday-Saturday: 7.30am –11pm; Sunday: 8.30am-10.30pm*
Food: *Monday-Saturday: Until 10pm, every day*
&

☎ *020 7402 2441*

Paddington tube and rail, buses 23, 27, 36, 7, 15, SL1, Sl2, N18, N23 and N36
Beers: *Fuller's London Pride, ESB and Chiswick Bitter are available regularly. Guest ales include Fuller's seasonal ales plus a variety from different breweries, including Hop Back, Morrells, Wychwood, Cotleigh, Smiles, Brain's and Exmoor.*

The licensee says 'we have a very surprising amount of locals for a station pub, who pop in for a pint or two after work' and it's not hard to see why, particularly if they're real ale lovers.

Although it's a Fuller's pub, the publican has an innovative policy of choosing regularly changing guest ales from breweries that are on the train routes from the station. Clearly his original idea pays dividends as, when we visited, someone on virtually every table was drinking hand pumped beer.

The pub's décor is fairly standard issue, with tiled and wooden floors, lots of decorative plasterwork, glass screens, brass light fittings, a plethora of chairs and tables and a raised non-smoking area. It's also noisy, with loud piped music, but then what do you expect from a station concourse pub?

Food features bangers and mash, chicken and avocado ciabatta, mushroom stroganoff, penne pasta and Moroccan feta and cous cous salad. For weary, hungry travellers, there's also a full English breakfast, with a vegetarian alternative, before 11am Monday to Saturday and up to mid-day on Sunday.

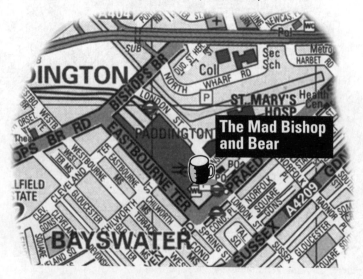

The Royal Exchange

26 Sale Place, Paddington

Open: *Monday-Friday: 11-11; Saturday: 11-4 and Sunday: 12-4*
Food: *Monday-Friday: All day; Sat and Sunday: 12-3*

❀ ☞

☎ *020 7723 3781*

Paddington or Edgware Road tube and rail, buses 8, 16, 6, 15 and 27
Beers: *Brakspear's Bitter and Boddingtons are available regularly, plus occasional guests.*

A Grade II listed building, this small, homely and welcoming free house reveals its authentic Irish roots with a large mirror emblazoned with 'Murphy's Stout' across the back wall, the odd picture of Jackie Charlton and, to cap it all, the Saw Doctors belting out one of their minor hits on the jukebox.

A love of horse racing is also very much in evidence – from the cartoons and prints of horses, jockeys and their supporters, like the Queen Mum, dotted around the walls to the punters quietly studying the form before placing their bets. But it's all good-natured and friendly stuff and those not involved in picking a winner are greeted as smilingly as those who beat a well-trodden path to the bookies each day.

Food is all home made, comes in legendarily large portions and includes roast beef, roast turkey, home cooked ham, pies and homemade vegetarian pizzas.

The Victoria

10a Strathern Place, Paddington

Open: *Monday-Friday: 11-11; Saturday: 12-11 and Sunday: 12-10.30*
Food: *Monday-Saturday: 12-2.30 and 6-10; Sunday: 12-4 and 6-9*

♿ ❀ ☞ *before 6pm*

☎ *020 7724 1191*

Lancaster Gate and Paddington tube and rail
Beers: *Fuller's London Pride, ESB and Chiswick are available regularly. Guest beers include Fuller's seasonal ales.*

A few minutes walk from Hyde Park, this pub is the Victoria, by name and by nature. Everything – from its theatrical velvet drapes, ornately carved dark wood, heavily gilded glass and brass globe light fittings – has a Victorian feel. The picture is completed with a painting of the formidable monarch and her beloved Prince Albert, surrounded by their children, displayed above one of the two open fireplaces.

Upstairs is a separate function room, called the theatre bar, as the original fittings were taken from London's Gaiety Theatre – which perhaps might be considered ironic, given the Queen's marked inability to be amused. In contrast, for those who crave light entertainment, there is a pub quiz on Tuesday evenings, auction nights and live sports shown on big screen television. Food includes fish and chips, bangers and mash and penne pasta with olives and sun dried tomatoes.

W3

...also worth trying

Duke of York

86 Steyne Road, Acton (Acton Town tube)
This is a one bar back street traditional local, 'relying on good food, good beer and good company'. Karaoke is held on Thursday evening.

W4

The City Barge

27 Strand-on-the-Green, Chiswick

Open: *Monday-Saturday: 11-11; Sunday: 12-10.30*
Food: *All day, every day*
  ♿ ❀ ␎ Ⓟ
✆ *020 8994 2148*
Gunnersbury tube, Kew Bridge railway and buses 65, 391 and 237.
Beers: *Courage Best and Directors and Greene King IPA are available regularly. Guest ales include Charles Wells Bombardier, Morland's Old Speckled Hen and others.*
Although the original building was badly damaged during the blitz of WWII, its oldest parts can be traced back to 1484. A more contemporary claim to fame is that part of the Beatles' film, *Help,* was shot here.

Once known as the Navigator's Arms, it acquired its current name in the 19th century when the Lord Mayor of London's ceremonial barge was moored outside for the winter. The oldest part of the pub is dark with low ceilings and features storm doors to prevent flooding at high tides. There's also a less atmospheric new bar to be found up a flight of steps.

Food is served all day, every day and is a cut above the average. Particular highlights might be Moroccan lamb with minted cous cous, steak and Stilton pie, home made 'barge' burgers, roasted red pepper lasagne, five bean chilli and a range of sandwiches and salads.

...also worth trying

Bell and Crown

72 Strand-on-the-Green, Chiswick (Gunnersbury Park tube/Kew Bridge railway)
This is an appealing riverside pub, with a conservatory area and no smoking room, serving Fuller's beers.

George and Devonshire

8 Burlington Lane, Chiswick (Turnham Green tube)

Close to the home of the English painter William Hogarth and next door to Fuller's brewery, the food is homemade and features authentic curries.

W5

The Red Lion

13 St Mary's Road, Ealing

Open: Monday-Saturday: 11-11; Sunday: 12-10.30
Food: Monday-Sunday: 12-2.30 and 6-9
❀ ☎ *only in the garden*
☎ *020 8567 2544*
South Ealing or Ealing Broadway tube and bus 65
***Beers:** Fuller's Chiswick Bitter, London Pride and ESB are available regularly. Seasonal ales are also from Fuller's brewery.*

Known locally as Stage Six, the Red Lion is opposite Ealing studios, home of the famous British comedies, and once the favoured watering hole of assorted luvvies and their hangers-on. When Sir Alec Guinness was called to take his place on the great stage set in the sky, the television cameras came here to record reactions to the news of his death.

A Grade II listed building, on top of the roof is a statue of a red lion. Inside, film memorabilia jostles with black and white stills of Jack Hawkins, Jack Warner, Dennis Price and others to adorn the walls of this compact, L-shaped room. A Fuller's pub, food includes Welsh rarebit, a selection of burgers, including vegetarian, and assorted sandwiches.

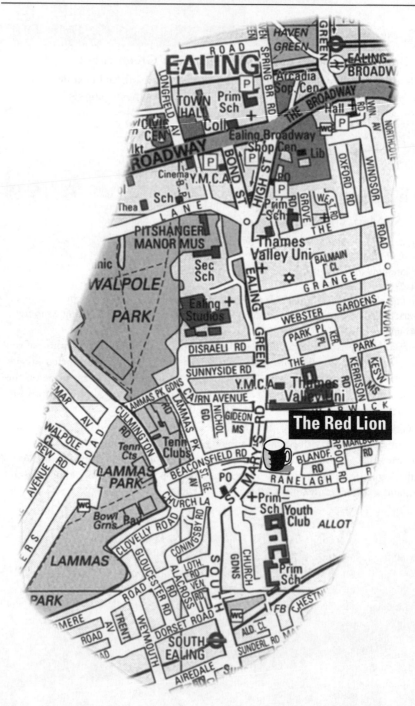

...also worth trying

Duffy's

124 Pitshanger Lane, Ealing (Hanger Lane tube)
This is a small, comfortable pub in a converted shop, selling a good range of real ales, including Hancock's HB, Fuller's and Young's. There's a restaurant at the rear.

W6

The Black Lion

2 South Black Lion Lane, Hammersmith

Open: Monday-Saturday: 12-11; Sunday: 12-10.30
Food: Monday-Sunday: 12-9.30
        ♿ ❀ ☎ ℗
☎ *020 8748 2639*
Stamford Brook tube
Beers: *Courage Best, Greene King IPA and Theakston's Old Peculiar. Guest ales may be introduced in the future.*

For those of us who are strangely moved by trees, it's worth visiting the Black Lion just to sit in the patio garden overlooking the Thames and admire the huge, imposing and more than 1, 000 year-old horse chestnut, with its knarred trunk.

The pub itself is a mere 200 years old and was originally a piggery, until the farmer decided to try his hand at brewing. His ales proved so popular that barrels soon replaced the pigs. Sadly one evening in 1804, excise officer Francis Smith supped a few tankards too many, and shot hapless builder, Thomas Millwood with his blunderbuss, after mistaking him for the Hammersmith Ghost.

Set at the west end of the Hammersmith Thames side pubs, the Black Lion is L-shaped and features high back wooden settles and beams. On the left and down a couple of stairs is the aptly named Long Room, where you'll find a pool table. On Thursday evenings there's a regular quiz.

There's a mixed crowd, including a few tourists, locals and those taking a break from their riverbank meanderings. An ideal venue for families, there's an adjacent children's play area and some food comes in child-sized portions. The adult menu features the usual pub staples, like steak and ale pie, lasagne, burgers and cheese and pasta broccoli bake. One minor suggestion: the pervasive and slightly off-putting smell of fried food might be cured by an investment in a better extraction system.

The Blue Anchor

13 Lower Mall, Hammersmith Bridge

Open: Monday-Saturday: 11-11; Sunday: 12-10.30
Food: Monday-Saturday: 12-2.30 and 6-9; Sunday: 12-3.30
& ⊛ ♨
☎ 020 8748 5774
Hammersmith Broadway tube
Beers: Young's Special, Courage Best and Directors are available regularly. Guests include Young's Winter Warmer, Wadworth 6X, Greene King Abbot Ale and Theakston's Old Peculiar.

Step inside this small one-room pub, which was first licensed in 1722, and you'll need to find your sea legs, as the rowing theme abounds. There are two boats fixed to the ceiling, anchors, helmets and a variety of other associated paraphernalia. On the day we visited, there was even a chap in a striped rowing blazer propping up the bar.

Next-door is the Auriol Kensington Rowing Club, who apparently won the Olympic sculls in 1912, and the patio overlooking the Thames offers a fine vantage point to view the springtime spectacle of the Oxford versus Cambridge University boat race.

There's lots of seating provided by padded benches – blue of course – wooden stools and chairs, but be warned you'll be lucky to bag one in the summer months, as the pub gets very busy. The half wooden panelled walls are covered with photographs and prints of Hammersmith Bridge, which is 200 yards away. Indeed, it's all so picturesque that it's often used as a film location, most recently in the movie, *Sliding Doors*. Another claim to fame is that the composer, Holst, wrote his *Hammersmith Suite* here.

Food is all home made and includes roasts of the day, chicken Veronique, mushroom stroganoff and spicy tomato tagliatelle.

The Dove

19 Upper Mall, Hammersmith Bridge

Open: *Monday-Saturday: 11-11; Sunday: 12-10.30*
Food: *Monday-Saturday: 12-2 and 6-9; Sunday: 12-4 and 6-9*
✿
☎ *020 8748 5405*
Hammersmith Broadway tube
Beers: *Fuller's London Pride and ESB are available regularly.*

Appearing in the Guinness Book of Records for having the smallest public bar, the Dove is a 17th century riverside pub with a list of past regulars worthy of *Who's Who*.

Apparently Charles II and Nell Gwynne drank here together, the poet James Thomson composed that tune so beloved of Tory Party conference delegates, *Rule Britannia*, in one of its upper rooms and Ernest Hemmingway and Graham

Greene were both to be found imbibing a snifter or two on the premises, when not crafting their novels.

Set in a narrow alley, the split-level pub has been owned by the Fuller's brewery since 1796, when it was called The Dove Coffee House. After several decades of being known as The Doves – the artist mistakenly painted the plural form on the sign – it reverted to its original name in 1948.

Walk through the door and the tiny public bar is off to your immediate right, where you'll find a brass plaque showing the level the floodwaters reached in 1928. In the main area, there's an open fireplace, copper topped tables, bare floorboards, beams and seating on wooden chairs and benches for no more than a dozen-and-a-half customers. On the day we visited, the room was so cosy and warm that the gentleman on the next table fell asleep over his pint, much to the irritation of the bar staff, who unceremoniously disturbed his slumbers.

Watch your head as you step up a few stairs to a second larger room, which also features an open fire and more seating. Beyond this you'll find a pleasant modern glass conservatory and terrace overlooking the Thames.

Food is all home made on the premises and includes steak and kidney pie, Cajun chicken, nachos grande, vegetable jalfrezi and lasagne.

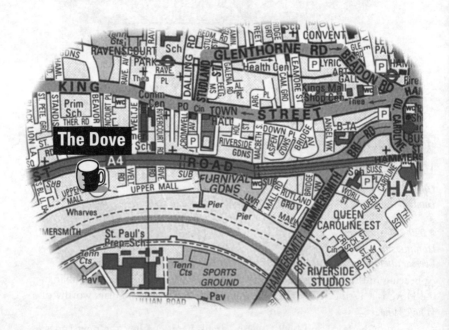

Thatched House

115 Dalling Road, Hammersmith

Open: Monday-Saturday: 11-3 and 5.30-11; Sunday: 12-10.30
Food: Monday-Saturday: 12-2.30 and 7-10; Sunday: 12-3.30 and 7-9.30
& ❀ ☕
☎ 020 8748 6174
Ravenscourt Park tube
Beers: Young's Bitter, Special and Triple A.

The brightly painted Thatched House stands out like a beacon in the otherwise drab urban landscape of this part of Hammersmith.

And the yellow theme continues inside this spacious and airy pub, although the vibrancy has been toned down a little and a muted green added. High ceilings, rug-covered floorboards, large vases of fresh flowers, an open fireplace and bits of modern art – including a portrait of Frank Sinatra – add to the upmarket feel. Service from the young and enthusiastic bar staff is excellent.

Food is similarly a cut above the rest and regularly features bangers and mash, rib-eye steak and roast field mushrooms. My celeriac soup, served with what looked like half a loaf of bread, was tasty and very good value, while my mate Dolly, who knows about these things, pronounced her gnocchi with smoked salmon "better than the Oxo Tower". Now that's rare praise indeed.

...also worth trying

Salutation

154 King Street, Hammersmith (Ravenscourt Park/Hammersmith Broadway tube)
This is a spacious and comfortable Edwardian one-room Fuller's pub, with a handsome tiled exterior, looking onto the High Street and opposite the town hall. There's a large conservatory and award-winning beer garden. Apparently the Queen mum visited in 1989.

W7

...also worth trying

The Fox Inn

Green Lane, Hanwell (Boston Manor tube)
A free house, built in 1853 and close to the Grand Union Canal and local conservation area, this pub offers an impressive range of ales including Fuller's London Pride, Brakspear's and Timothy Taylor's Landlord. There's a quiz on Thursdays and occasional music mid-week.

W8

Windsor Castle

114 Campden Hill Road, Notting Hill

Open: Monday-Saturday: 12-11.30; Sunday: 12-11
Food: Monday-Saturday: 12-10.30; Sunday: 12-4 and 5-10
& ❀
☎ 020 7243 9551
Notting Hill Gate tube
Beers: *Bass and Fuller's London Pride are available regularly.*

A short stroll from Portobello Market, the Windsor Castle was built in 1850 and has three dark-wood-paneled bars with lots of intimate booths.

Politicians jostle with actors and Notting Hill's upmarket set for space at the crowded bar, which is overlooked by a positive rogues' gallery of former famous punters who have left behind their calling card: a signed photograph. There's a walled and paved garden at the pub's rear that proves extremely popular in the summer months.

Apparently the name derives from that fact that before the area was developed, it was possible to see the Berkshire castle from an upstairs window. Today it just has to make do with its proximity to Kensington Palace.

Food includes sausage and mash, mussels and garlic in cream sauce, fish and chips, homemade pesto pasta and roasted Mediterranean vegetable ciabatta.

...also worth trying

The Britannia

1 Allen Street, Kensington (Kensington High Street tube)
This traditional, friendly local, just off Kensington High Street, and serving Young's beers has the prestigious distinction of featuring in every edition of CAMRA's *Good Beer Guide*.

Churchill Arms

119 Kensington Church Street (Notting Hill tube)
A multi award winning 1930s Fuller's pub, stuffed with memorabilia relating to the cigar-smoking wartime leader.
There's an acclaimed Thai restaurant in the conservatory.

Old Pack Horse

434 Chiswick High Road (Chiswick Park tube)
This is an imposing Fuller's pub, opposite the green, with three main drinking areas and recommended Thai food in the restaurant.

Scarsdale

23A Edwardes Square (Kensington High Street tube)
This is a lovely, upmarket pub in an even lovelier square.

Uxbridge Arms

13 Uxbridge Street (Notting Hill Gate tube)
Try this one if you yearn for a quiet pub with old world charm, decent beer and some interesting characters.

W9

Warrington Hotel

93 Warrington Crescent, Maida Vale

Open: Monday-Saturday: 11-11 and Sunday: 12-10.30
Food: Monday-Sunday: 12-2.30 and 6-10.30
❀ ☙
☎ *020 7286 2929*
Maida Vale and Warwick Avenue tube, bus 16
Beers: Fuller's London Pride and ESB, Young's Special and Brakspear Special are available regularly. There are regular guest ales.

Set in an area of London where the hired help is regularly seen out walking their mistresses' prize pooches, the Warrington Hotel is as plush and grand as you might imagine an upper crust local to be. That many years ago it served as a brothel is perhaps something that the great and good of Maida Vale feel is best forgotten.

Built in 1859, the wide steps and elaborate tiled and mosaic exterior, lead to a luxurious interior featuring an ornately painted ceiling, deep alcoves, marble pillars, red upholstery and an enormous semi-circular, marble topped bar. There is a Thai restaurant, which offers vegetarian alternatives.

W14

The Colton Arms

187 Greyhound Road, Barons Court

Open: Monday-Friday: 11.30-3 and 5.30-11; Saturday: 11.30-4 and 7 to 11; Sunday: 12-4
and 7-10.30
Food: Monday-Saturday: 12-2.30
& ❀
☎ 020 7385 6956
West Hammersmith or Barons Court tube
Beers: Young's Best, Greene King IPA, Courage Directors and Shepherd Neame Spitfire
are available regularly.

Originally built in 1790, the Colton Arms is behind the Queen's Club tennis
courts in Kensington. Small and cosy, there's an attractive horseshoe shaped copper bar, with one room at the front and two tiny but aptly named 'snug' bars.

Three fireplaces, antique carved wooden furniture, brass ornaments and plates on
the walls complete the village pub atmosphere, which is enhanced by the lack of
intrusive television screens, music and gaming machines. A selection of bar snacks
is available at lunchtimes from Monday to Saturday.

The Warwick Arms

160 Warwick Road, Kensington

Open: M-Saturday: 12-11; Sunday: 12-10.30
Food: Monday-Friday: 12-3 and 6-10; Saturday: 12-3; Sunday: 10-4
& ❀ *Ch: Only if eating*
☎ 020 7603 3560
Earl's Court or Olympia tube
Beers: Fuller's London Pride and ESB and Adnams are available regularly.

Dating from 1828 and just around the corner from Olympia Exhibition Centre,
the Warwick Arms is a popular watering hole for those visiting CAMRA's annual
Great British Beer Festival, held in the summer.

Décor features exposed brick walls at one end of the pub, with a stone floor
while the other has wood panelled walls and bare floorboards. There are two fireplaces, one with a leather chesterfield, and lots of bric-a-brac hanging from the
ceiling and walls. Some of the bar stools are made of painted milk churns. There's
a small covered beer garden at the rear.

Beer quality has received recognition from both Cask Marque and Fuller's brewery. Popular food choices include a chicken and bacon club sandwich, cod in real
ale batter, homemade pies, cream cheese and broccoli bake and pasta pomodoro.

BRENTFORD

Brewery Tap

47 Catherine Wheel Road, TW8

Open: Monday-Saturday: 11-11; Sunday: 12-10.30
Food: Monday-Friday: 12-2.45; Saturday: Match days only; Sunday: 12-2.30
✿
☎ 020 8560 5200

Brentford railway, Boston Manor tube and buses 237, 235 and E8
Beers: Fuller's ESB, London Pride, Chiswick Bitter plus seasonal Fuller's Ales including Jack Frost, Summer Ale, Honey Dew and Red Fox.

Close to Syon Park and Gardens and the Grand Union Canal, the Brewery Tap boasts the unusual attribute of being raised above street level to avoid flooding.

You'd expect a pub with this name to have a brewery nearby – and once upon a time you would have been right. The William Gomm brewery was bought by Fullers in 1908, but subsequently shut down.

A lively local with three small bars, there's free live jazz every Tuesday and Thursday, a duo on Friday and Sunday and a pianist on Saturday. A quiz is held every Monday evening. Food includes ham, egg and chips, scampi, cheese and vegetable bakes and a daily special, Monday to Friday. Food is only served on Saturdays when Brentford FC is playing at home at nearby Griffin Park. Booking is advisable for Sunday lunch.

The Magpie and Crown

128 High Street, TW8

Open: Monday-Saturday: 11-11; Sunday: 12-10.30
Food: Monday-Friday: 11-2.30 and 5.30-7.30.
✿
☎ 020 8560 5658

Brentford railway and buses 237, 235, 267, E2 and E8
Beers: A regularly changing list of four beers, often featuring Brakspear's Bitter and Greene King IPA. The pub also stocks a wide variety of bottle conditioned and continental beers.

A local CAMRA pub of the year, the Magpie and Crown is a beer drinkers' haven, with a regularly changing list of four well-tended and reasonably priced ales, often including more unusual choices from microbreweries and independents. Indeed, landlord Stephen Bolton says that they've offered more than 800 beers in the last five years.

Built in 1923 in mock Tudor style, you'll find this friendly High Street local opposite the magistrates' court. On Friday evening there is karaoke and an occasional quiz night. Food includes chilli con carne, jacket potatoes and assorted sandwiches and toasties.

CRANFORD

Queens Head

123 High Street, TW5

Open: *Monday-Saturday: 11-11; Sunday: 12-10.30*
Food: *Monday-Saturday: 12-3 and 6-9; Sunday: 12-3*
  ♿ ❀ ☕ Ⓟ
☎ *020 8897 0722*
Heathrow tube and buses 111 and H28
Beers: *Fuller's Chiswick, ESB and London Pride plus seasonal Fuller's Ales including Jack Frost, Summer Ale, Honey Dew and Red Fox.*

The first pub to hold a license to sell spirits, the Queen's Head was once the haunt of highwaymen but was rebuilt last century in mock Tudor style. A past regular in CAMRA's *Good Beer Guide*, the pub has one bar that serves two distinct drinking areas. The home made food includes steak and ale or chicken and mushroom pie, lamb's liver and bacon, risotto and broccoli and Stilton bake.

GREENFORD

Black Horse

425 Oldfield Lane, UB6

Open: *Monday-Saturday: 11.30-11.30; Sunday: 12-10.30*
Food: *Monday-Saturday: 12-9.30; Sunday: 12-9*
  ♿ ❀ ☕ Ⓟ
☎ *020 8578 1384*
Greenford tube and bus 92
Beers: *Fuller's ESB and London Pride plus seasonal Fuller's Ales including Jack Frost, Summer Ale, Honey Dew and Red Fox.*

Step down from the lounge into the large beer garden, with its wooden terrace overlooking the bend of the Grand Union Canal, and immediately you feel transported to the countryside, leaving the urban landscape far behind – yet you're just two minutes walk from the local tube station.

Busy and friendly, the Black Horse also provides a consistently good pint of Fuller's ales, as its inclusion in many editions of CAMRA's *Good Beer Guide* proves. Food includes London Pride battered cod, steak and ale pie, jacket potatoes, roasted vegetable Wellington with port and Stilton sauce and red onion and Stilton tart.

HAMPTON COURT

The King's Arms

Lion Gate, Hampton Court Road, East Molesley, Surrey

Open: Monday-Saturday: 11-11; Sunday: 12-10.30
Food: Monday-Sunday: 12-8
 ♿ ❀ ♋ Ⓟ
☎ 020 8977 1729
Hampton Court railway and buses 111, 172, 246
Beers: *Badger Best Bitter, Tanglefoot and Sussex Ale are available regularly. Guests might include King and Barnes Winter Old Ale and Badger Golden Champion.*

The last time I visited the King's Arms, I was still smarting from the embarrassment of being lost in Hampton Court Palace's legendary maze – indeed I'd probably still be there now, if my better half hadn't taken pity and decided to use his bat-like sense of direction to find the way out. Thankfully, it was nothing that a very welcome pint of Badger's beer in this historic and imposing pub couldn't put right.

Apparently once a 'house of disrepute' for Henry VIII, the pub features a series of panels depicting his six wives. There are three bars, one with a darts board and bar billiards, and other entertainment includes live blues and jazz once a month. Food veers towards traditional English and includes fish and chips, chicken arrabiata and roast beef and Yorkshire pudding.

HAMPTON HILL

...also worth trying

Roebuck

72 Hampton Road, Hampton Hill (Fulwell railway)
Local CAMRA members have given their thumbs up to this comfortable corner free house, saying that it's a "good revival of what used to be one of the worst pubs in our area". Badger Best Bitter is always available, plus a guest beer that changes each month.

HOUNSLOW

The Cross Lances

236 Hanworth Road, TW3

Open: Monday-Saturday: 11-11; Sunday: 12-10.30
Food: Monday-Friday: 12-3 and 6-9; Sat and Sunday: 12-5

☎ 020 8570 4174
Hounslow railway and Hounslow Central tube
Beers: Fuller's ESB and London Pride plus seasonal Fuller's Ales including Jack Frost, Summer Ale, Honey Dew and Red Fox.

This family orientated pub hosts a barbeque with live music every Bank Holiday Monday afternoon in its award-winning garden. An early Victorian friendly and hospitable local, there's a quiz every Thursday and live music at the weekends. Food is served in large portions and includes homemade Lancashire hotpot, roast of the day served with a giant Yorkshire pudding, seafood pasta in a tomato, garlic and chilli sauce and a hot and spicy vegetable curry. The landlord has received planning permission for a restaurant extension – but currently it's still worth booking, especially for Sunday lunch.

ISLEWORTH

The Coach and Horses

183 London Road TW7

Open: Monday-Saturday: 11-Midnight; Sunday: 12-10.30
Food: Monday-Saturday: 12-2.30 and 6-10; Sunday: 12-4

☎ 020 8560 1447
Syon Lane railway, Hounslow East tube and buses 235, 267, H28 and 237.
Beers: Young's Bitter, Special and Triple A. Guests are from Young's brewery.

This 17th century coaching inn, on the edge of Syon Park, is mentioned in Charles Dickens' *Oliver Twist* and recommended in CAMRA's *Good Beer Guide* – the landlord is a member.

The pub stages live jazz and folk music on almost every day of the week, bar Thursday, when there's a quiz. On Monday, there is modern jazz; Tuesday has country and bluegrass sessions; there is an Irish session on Wednesday where musicians are welcome to join in; Friday has easy listening bands; Saturday offers rock and blues; and there's a live band on Sunday afternoon.

There's a friendly atmosphere, open fires in winter and a pretty family garden for the summer. Food is Thai, with the addition of a traditional lunch of roast beef and Yorkshire pudding offered on Sunday.

...also worth trying

Red Lion
92-94 Linkfield Road, Isleworth (Isleworth railway)
This large local, specialising in Brakspear's beers, is hidden away in a quiet terrace, with a sign advertising its presence at the end of an opposite alleyway. Close to the station, there's live music Saturday evenings and Sunday lunchtimes.

SOUTHALL

Beaconsfield Arms

63–67 West End Road, UB1
Open: Monday-Saturday: 11-11; Sunday: 12-10.30
Food: None
& ❀ ☛ *daytime only;* Ⓟ
☎ *020 8574 8135*
Southall railway and buses 207 and 607
Beers: Greene King Abbot Ale, Scanlon's Spike and Ansell's Mild are available regularly. There are regularly changing guest ales.

There aren't too many London pubs where you will find Ansell's Mild regularly on offer, but the Beaconsfield Arms is one of them. Unusually situated halfway down a residential street, but not visible from either end, this campaigning, basically decorated local also offers a changing menu of interesting ales from a variety of small independent breweries, like the Marlow-based Rebellion Beer Company. There's no food, but you can easily find a good curry in the Broadway nearby.

TEDDINGTON

The Queen Dowager

49 North Lane, Teddington

Open: Monday-Saturday: 11-11; Sunday: 12-10.30
Food: Lunchtime Monday to Sat but hours will be extended during 2001 – check with the pub for more details
❀ ☘ *only in the garden*
☎ 020 8977 2583
Teddington railway and buses 281, 285, 33, R68.
Beers: Young's Bitter, Special and Triple A. Guests are from Young's brewery.

Although it's under new management, following the retirement of a longstanding landlord, the Queen Dowager retains its reputation as a pleasant, quiet local serving well-kept Young's Ales. Food is home-cooked and includes steak and Guinness pie, gammon, pasta, mushroom stroganoff and cauliflower cheese.

TWICKENHAM

The Eel Pie

9-11 Church Street, Twickenham

Open: Monday-Saturday: 11-11; Sunday: 12-10.30
Food: Monday-Saturday: 12-9; Sunday: 12-6
☘
☎ 020 8891 1717
Twickenham railway and tube and buses R68, R70, 33 and 281.
Beers: Badger Best, IPA and Tanglefoot are all available regularly. Guests might include Marston's Pedigree, Timothy Taylor's Landlord, Brakspear's Best and Morland's Old Speckled Hen.

This popular Twickenham pub started life as a collection of three town houses that were knocked through to form a single bar. A cobbled street and a pretty, pastel coloured exterior leads to an interior featuring a rugby theme – not entirely unexpected, given its proximity to the home of English rugby.

Part of the pub was once a funeral parlour, with the mortuary now functioning as the cellar cold room. The name comes from the Eel Pie Hotel, on Eel Pie Island in the Thames. Famous in the swinging sixties as a hotbed of sex and drugs and rock n' roll, the hotel has gone now, but its name lives on in the pub sign. Today, entertainment is a rather more sombre affair of a pub quiz on Tuesday evenings, held to raise money for the pub's football and cricket teams.

Food includes chilli, smoked haddock and mashed potato, homemade pies, pasta with mushrooms and cream, stir-fry vegetables and baked potatoes. As the landlord proudly says: "It's the kind of pub that you introduce people to with a smug grin, because you know it's going to be okay."

UXBRIDGE

Load of Hay

33 Villier Street UB8

Open: Monday-Friday: 11-3 and 5.30-11; Saturday: 11-3 and 7-11; Sunday: 12-3 and 7-10.30
Food: Monday-Fri: 12-2.30 and 6-9; Saturday: 12-2.30 and 7-9.30; Sunday: 12-2.30
& ❀ ☎ ℗
☎ 01895 234676
Uxbridge tube and buses U3, 207 and 222.
Beers: Crown Buckley Best Bitter is regularly available plus two or three others that might include beers from Cottage Brewery, Wye Valley, O'Hanlons, Rebellion, Everards and others.

A traditional beamed pub close to Brunel University, the Load of Hay wins loads of praise for the quality of its ales – many of which come from microbreweries – and good value home-cooked food. There's a warm welcome for everyone in this comfortable local, with the over-60s offered a 20 per cent discount on meals. Options include steak pie, chicken curry, lasagne, quiche, pasta and stir fries. There's an occasional pub quiz but no jukebox or pool tables. One note of caution: it's three-quarters of a mile from the nearest tube station. So pack your walking shoes.

WEST DRAYTON

De Burgh Arms Hotel

Station Approach, High Street, UB7

Open: *Monday-Friday: 12-11; Saturday: 11-11; Sunday: 12-10.30*
Food: *Monday-Saturday: 12-9.45; Sunday: 12-6.45*
&. ❀ ℗
☎ *01895 432823*
West Drayton railway and buses U1, U3 and 222.
Beers: *Tetley Bitter, Marston's Pedigree, plus a regularly changing guest ale and Adnams Broadside are available.*

A 17th century Grade II listed building, this large pub is most famous for its appearance in the classic British film *Genevieve*. Next door to the station, food includes haddock and chips and Cajun chicken.

ALPHABETICAL INDEX OF PUBS

The CAMRA Books range of guides helps you search out the best in beer (and cider) and brew it at home too!

Buying in the UK

All our books are available through bookshops in the UK. If you can't find a book, simply order it from your bookshop using the ISBN number, title and author details given below. CAMRA members should refer to their regular monthly newspaper What's Brewing for the latest details and member special offers. CAMRA books are also available by mail-order (postage free) from: CAMRA Books, 230 Hatfield Road, St Albans, Herts, AL1 4LW. Cheques made payable to CAMRA Ltd. Telephone your credit card order on 01727 867201.

Buying outside the UK

CAMRA books are also sold in many book and beer outlets in the USA and other English-speaking countries. If you have trouble locating a particular book, use the details below to order with your credit card (or US$ cheque) by mail, email (info@camra.org.uk), fax (+44 1727 867670) or web site. The web site (www.camra.org.uk) will securely process credit card purchases.

Carriage of £3.00 per book (Europe) and £6.00 per book (US, Australia, New Zealand and other overseas) is charged.

UK Booksellers

Call CAMRA Books for distribution details and book list. CAMRA Books are listed on all major CD-ROM book lists and on our Internet site: http://www.camra.org.uk

Overseas Booksellers

Call or fax CAMRA Books for details of local distributors.

Distributors are required for some English language territories and rights are available for electronic and non-English language editions. Enquiries should be addressed to the managing editor (mark-webb@msn.com).

CAMRA Guides

Painstakingly researched and checked, these guides are the leaders in their field, bringing you to the door of pubs which serve real ale and more...

CAMRA's Good Cider Guide

by David Matthews

400 pages **Price: £9.99**

CAMRA's guide to real cider researched anew for the new Millennium and now with features on cider around the world – North America, France, Spain.

The guide contains three main sections:

Features on cider-making from around the world, bottled cider and cider traditions.

○ A comprehensive and detailed guide to UK producers of cider. Each producer entry includes details of the ciders produced, availability, cost, and visitor information. There are also notes on the producer's cider-making background and history. All this data is newly surveyed by the editor and a huge team of CAMRA volunteers.

○ A brand new listing of outlets – pubs, restaurants, bars, small cider makers – with full address including postcode and telephone contact numbers. Details of ciders available and, where appropriate, items of interest in the pub or area.

Use the following code to order this book from your bookshop:
ISBN 1-85249-143-4

Room at the Inn 2nd edition

by Jill Adam

324 pages **Price: £8.99**

This second edition of the hugely popular Room at the Inn is your guide to quality overnight accommodation with a decent selection of real ale for good measure. The guide has been completely resurveyed and researched from scratch by the grass roots experts of the Campaign for Real Ale. Each entry in the guide gives local directions, contact details, opening times, type and extent of accommodation, list of beers, meal types and times, easy to understand price guide and snippets about local attractions and the sometimes centuries-old tales associated with your resting place.

Use the following code to order this book from your bookshop:
ISBN 1-85249-150-7

Heritage Pubs of Great Britain

by Mark Bolton and James Belsey

144 pages hard back   Price: £16.99

It is still possible to enjoy real ale in sight of great craftsmanship and skill. What finer legacy for today's drinkers? Feast your eyes and toast the architects and builders from times past. This full colour collectible is a photographic record of some of the finest pub interiors in Britain. Many of the pubs included have been chosen from CAMRA's national inventory of pub interiors which should be saved at all costs. As a collector's item, it is presented on heavy, gloss-art paper in a sleeved hard back format. The pub interiors have been photographed by architectural specialist Mark Bolton and described in words by pub expert James Belsey. Available only from CAMRA – call 01727 867201 (overseas +44 1727 867201)

Pubs for Families

by David Perrott

308 pages   Price: £8.99

Traditional pubs with CAMRA-approved ale and a warm welcome for the kids! Nothing could be better. But where to find such a hospitable hostel on home patch, let alone when out and about or on holiday? *Pubs for Families* contains invaluable national coverage with easy to use symbols so that you know what facilities are available and regional maps so you'll know how to get there. Get the best of both worlds with this invaluable guide.

Use the following code to order this book from your bookshop: ISBN 1-85249-141-8

Good Pub Food 5th edition

by Susan Nowak

448 pages approx   Price: £9.99

The pubs in these pages serve food as original and exciting as anything available in far more expensive restaurants. And, as well as the exotic and unusual, you will find landlords and landladies serving simple, nourishing pub fare such as a genuine ploughman's lunch or a steak and kidney pudding.

Award-winning food and beer writer Susan Nowak, who has travelled the country to complete this fifth edition of the guide, says that 'eating out' started in British inns and taverns and this guide is a contribution to an appreciation of all that is best in British food…and real cask conditioned ale.

Use the following code to order this book from your bookshop: ISBN 1-85249-151-5

50 Great Pub Crawls

by Barrie Pepper

256 pages   Price: £9.99

Visit the beer trails of the UK, from town centre walks, to hikes and bikes and a crawl on a train on which the pubs are even situated on your side of the track!

Barrie Pepper, with contributions and recommendations from CAMRA branches, has compiled a 'must do' list of pub crawls, with easy to use colour maps to guide you, notes on architecture, history and brewing tradition to entertain you.

Use the following code to order this book from your bookshop:
ISBN 1-85249-142-6

Good Beer Guides

These are comprehensive guides researched by professional beer writers and CAMRA enthusiasts. Use these guides to find the best beer on your travels or to plan your itinerary for the finest drinking. Travel and accommodation information, plus maps, help you on your way and there's plenty to read about the history of brewing, the beer styles and the local cuisine to back up the entries for bars and beverages.

Good Beer Guide to Belgium, Holland and Luxembourg

by Tim Webb

286 pages   Price: £9.99

Discover the stunning range and variety of beers available in the Low Countries, our even nearer neighbours via Le Tunnel. Channel-hopping Tim Webb's latest edition – the third – of the guide offers even more bars in which an incredible array of beers can be enjoyed. There are maps, tasting notes, beer style guide and a beers index to complete the most comprehensive companion to drinking with your Belgian and Dutch hosts.

Use the following code to order this book from your bookshop:
ISBN 1-85249-139-6

Good Beer Guide to Northern France

by Arthur Taylor

256 pages   Price: £7.99

Discover the excitement of the bars and cafes, the tranquillity of the village breweries which hold the secrets of generations of traditional brewing. Join the many festivals and cultural events such as the beer-refreshed second-hand market in Lille and the presentation of the Christmas ales. Find out where the best beer meets the best mussels and chips. Cuisine à la bière and more! Arthur Taylor is a leading authority on French beer and a member of Les Amis de la Bière, who have co-operated in the research for this book.

Use the following code to order this book from your bookshop:
ISBN 1-85249-140-X

Good Bottled Beer Guide

by Jeff Evans

128 pages   Price: £8.99

Now in its third edition, *Good Bottled Beer Guide* is becoming the complete *guide to buying bottle-conditioned beers*, including features on the main ingredients and identifying the flavours. When early nights and unfriendly traffic conspire to keep you at home, there's no risk these days of missing out on drinking a fine real ale. Britain's off-licences and supermarkets now stock bottle-conditioned ales – real ale in a bottle. The book lists all known bottle-conditioned beers and gives ingredients and tasting notes, plus contact information for out of the way producers.

Use the following code to order this book from your bookshop:
ISBN 1-85249-173-6

Good Beer Guide

edited by Roger Protz

750 pages approx   Price: £12.99

Produced annually in early October

Fancy a pint? Let CAMRA's *Good Beer Guide* lead the way. Revised each year to include around 5,000 great pubs serving excellent ale – country pubs, town pubs and pubs by the sea.

Fully and freshly researched by members of the Campaign for Real Ale, real enthusiasts who use the pubs week in, week out. No payment is ever taken for inclusion. The guide has location maps for each county and you can read full details of all Britain's breweries (big and small) and the ales they produce, including tasting notes.

Other Books

Cellarmanship

by Ivor Clissold

144 pages   Price: £6.99

This book explains every aspect of running a good cellar and serving a great pint of real ale which does both pub and brewer proud. It's a must have book for all professionals in the drinks trade, for all those studying at college to join it, and for all those who need to tap a cask of real ale for a party or beer festival.

Use the following code to order this book from your bookshop:
ISBN 1-85249-126-4

Dictionary of Beer

by CAMRA

168 pages   £7.99

This newly compiled dictionary contains thousands of definitions and descriptions to make it a unique specialist resource. The dictionary contains definitions of beer, brewing, tasting, alcohol and pub related terms. It also lists UK real ale breweries and well-known brewery names from around the world. The book is a useful purchase for individuals, institutions or businesses with an involvement in the huge drinks industry. Not to mention those who are interested in beer as a hobby or leisure interest.

Use the following code to order this book from your bookshop:
ISBN 1-85249-158-2

Brew Your Own

Learn the basics of brewing real ales at home from the experts. And then move on to more ambitious recipes which imitate well-loved ales from the UK and Europe.

Homebrew Classics – Indian Pale Ale

by Clive La Pensée and Roger Protz

Pages: 196 pages   Price: £8.99

The Homebrew Classics series tells you everything you need to know about particular beer styles. Indian Pale Ale provides the background knowledge about ingredients and technique so that you can can reproduce the style authentically with your homebrew equipment.

In order to create this series CAMRA has brought together the talents of home brewer Clive La Pensée and beer journalist Roger Protz. La Pensée brings the practical and technical knowhow and Protz delivers the knowledge of beer styles – their history, provenance and modern ingredients as commercially brewed.

The result is a collection of recipes which allow the home brewer to replicate the famous IPA style of cask-conditioned beer. Look out for the other titles in the series: Mild, Stout & Porter, Bitter and more.

Use the following code to order this book from your bookshop:

ISBN: 1-85249-129-9

Brew your own Real Ale at Home

by Graham Wheeler and Roger Protz

194 pages   Price: £8.99

This book contains recipes which allow you to replicate some famous cask-conditioned beers at home or to customise brews to your own particular taste.

Conversion details are given so that the measurements can be used world-wide.

Use the following code to order this book from your bookshop:

ISBN 1-85249-138-8

Brew Classic European Beers at Home

by Graham Wheeler and Roger Protz

196 pages   Price: £8.99

Keen home brewers can now recreate some of the world's classic beers. In your own home you can brew superb pale ales, milds, porters, stouts, Pilsners, Alt, Kolsch, Trappist, wheat beers, sour beers, even the astonishing fruit lambics of Belgium... and many more. Measurements are given in UK, US and European units, emphasising the truly international scope of the beer styles within.

Use the following code to order this book from your bookshop:
ISBN 1-85249-117-5

Home Brewing

by Graham Wheeler

240 pages   Price: £8.99

Recently redesigned to make it even easier to use, this is the classic first book for all home-brewers. While being truly comprehensive, Home Brewing also manages to be a practical guide which can be followed step by step as you try your first brews. Plenty of recipes for beginners and hints and tips from the world's most revered home brewer.

Use the following code to order this book from your bookshop:
ISBN 1-85249-137-X